CRICUT:

This Book Includes:

Cricut for Beginners; Cricut Design Space; Cricut Project Ideas. The Ultimate Guide for Beginners and Advanced Users for to Create Wonderful Objects Using your Cricut Machine.

JADE PAPER

THIS BOOK INCLUDES

BOOK 1: 10
CRICUT FOR BEGINNERS:

A Step-by-Step Beginner's Guide to Learn How to Master Your Cricut Machine, as a Hobby or to Make Money. Including Many Project Ideas, Practical Examples, Tips & Tricks.

BOOK 2: 120
CRICUT DESIGN SPACE:

The Ultimate Guide for Beginners and Advanced Users. Tools, Explore Air 2 and Design Space, Cricut Projects for all Levels, Tips & Tricks, Practical Examples and Much More.

BOOK 3: 260
CRICUT PROJECT IDEAS:

How to Create Wonderful Objects Using your Cricut Machine. A Step-by-Step Guide to Beginners and Advanced Amazing Projects; Including Practical Examples, Tips & Tricks.

CRICUT FOR

BEGINNERS:

A Step-by-Step Beginner's Guide to Learn How to Master Your Cricut Machin, as a Hobby or to Make Money. Including Many Project Ideas, Practical Examples, Tips & Tricks.

JADE PAPER

Table Of Contents

Introduction

Cricut may seem complicated at first, but there is a lot you can do with this machine – and a lot that you can get out of it. If you feel confused by Cricut, then take your time, get familiar with the buttons, and start having fun with it.

With Cricut, anything is possible. If you've been speculating what you can do with your machine, the simple answer is almost anything. For designers, for those who like to make precise cuts and for those who like to print their own shirts, this is a wonderful option to consider. If you are thinking of getting a Cricut machine, you'll see here that there is a lot that you can do with this unique tool, and endless creative possibilities.

Cricut has come a long way since it was first introduced in 2006 by Provo Craft & Novelty, Inc., and has undergone many changes. The company has released many versions of its die-cutting machine as its popularity among crafters has soared.

Cricut is a home die cutting machine that can be used for various art or craft work or projects like scrap booking and textiles. With the book, you would be taught and you would become familiar with the Cricut cutting machine and also learn how to create your own crafts. The first and original Cricut cutting machine was invented in the year 2006, the inventors had a pretty basic and simple idea: to give crafters a very easy way to create a very professional-looking paper crafts with a handmade feel. In 2014, an idea was inspired. The inventors wanted another machine so capable that it could inspire many more people to lead creative lives. In order to make this a reality, the inventors had to rethink and strategize everything. They created new tools and technologies, simplified the initial and original software, and added thousands of new project possibilities. And the result of this particular idea was the Cricut Maker. Cricut machines may be useful for different tasks. Their versatility and effectiveness make them popular with die-cutting options. That's why, particularly when you're a professional crafter, you need a Cricut machine. If you're a newbie, you'll find the best cutting machine multi-functional and easy to use.

Cricut Maker was the dream project. Whether you like to make things from scratch, or begin with things that has already been designed, your Cricut machine and Design Space software work together to make design easier.

From its inception, the Cricut has provided many ways for a crafter to make beautiful things and sell them for a nice profit.

Most of us, whether we're Cricut pros or a beginner, have seen the many items for sale at craft shows and in specialty stores. Everything from popular saying and quotes stenciled on wood signs to monogrammed water tumblers and most everything in between.

Some Cricut users have mastered the machine and they can make vinyl letters look as if they were painted onto the wood. The vinyl meshes so well that with the naked eye you won't be able to find a spot to lift one of the vinyl letters. That's how realistic it can look. And, most vinyls are weather-resistant. That means you can make all kinds of awesome things for outside as well as inside.

Cricut has come so far since the days of die-cutting for scrapbooking, and although scrapbooking is still popular, you don't see as many sheets of stickers in stores, and in some stores, the scrapbooking unit has shrunk since Cricut has become so much more than your scrapbooking partner.

And that's not to say scrapbooking isn't fun, but it is to say that ideas are endless and you can make almost anything you can think of.

Best of all, many Cricut models are Bluetooth enabled, making it easy to communicate with your other devices. The Cricut machine is any scrapbooker most confided in companion and partner. Scrapbooking goes connected at the hip with pictures. Back in the mid-nineteenth century, the formation of scrapbooks was an exceptionally unpredictable assignment, and individuals regarded the procedure. With the blast in innovation, things are currently significantly more agreeable to achieve on account of numerous instruments that are promptly accessible now, for example, the Cricut cutting machine.

What does a Cricut cutting machine do accurately? The Cricut is in charge of the printing of structures that can be utilized for your scrapbook. At the point when the idea of making an accumulation is still in its beginning times, we think about the topic for it. How about we take the case of a wedding. After setting up your Cricut machine according to the instruction, there will be directions on your screen that you must follow to create your first project. You will still be using the link you found on the paper when you were setting up your machine. If you have not yet received your machine and are interested in knowing how it works, or you are looking for extra clarifications

The sort of structure that you should think of must be something that reproduces the climate of the wedding and let the watcher travel back in time and remember what happened during that occasion. The Cricut, alongside a PC and programming apparatus called the Cricut structure studio, can enable you to accomplish that. Likewise, you can alter structures that you think would suit your scrapbook needs, thus substantially more.

CHAPTER 1:

Cricut Machine

While the brand envelops a few distinct items, including heat presses and embossers, the word Cricut has gotten synonymous with kick the bucket cutting machines. So in case, you're wondering, what is a Cricut machine? The appropriate response is a home pass on cutting machines utilized for papermaking and different expressions and specialties.

Basically, it's a savvy cutting machine known as the "flawless passage point to the universe of exactness making."

It's imperative to realize that these machines are not just utilized for cutting paper. They're made to cut a wide assortment of material in astonishing manners. Vinyl is another material that is related to kick the bucket cutting machines, just as felt, card stock, thus numerous others. They can even cut wood!

Notwithstanding cutting a wide range of materials, the machines that are presently accessible can likewise draw with pens, compose with pens, and score material for fresh, easy collapsing.

HOW TO BUY THE BEST MACHINE

Before you settle on the best model for you, you might need to consider a portion of the standard and extra highlights that a Cricut machine can offer you. This can incorporate different cutting rates, fluctuated material settings, extra tools, expanded scoring and composing capacities, various modifications and settings, remote ability, and even tool holders on the model itself.

Cutting velocity

Most Cricut machines will work at quick standard velocities, yet there are fresher models, for example, the Cricut explore air 2, or Cricut maker, which offer significantly quicker cutting occasions, as much as up to multiple times that of the standard models. Notwithstanding, a sped-up won't adjust the impacts of your projects or change the outcomes – it simply implies that you can accomplish more one after another.

A quicker machine will possibly truly be advantageous to you on the off chance that you have to traverse a great deal in one session, or on the off chance that you use it all the time for different projects, maybe even some expert.

Different types of Cricut machine

1. Cricut Maker – Editor's Choice

Highlights

•   Size: up to 12 x 24 inches

- Workable materials: 100+, from paper and texture to chipboard and balsa

- Writing: yes

- Scoring: yes

- Wireless: yes

The Cricut Maker machine makes the highest priority on the rundown, as this is considered a definitive in shrewd cutting machines. Unlike the Cricut explore air 2, this permits the slicing of up to 300 unique sorts of materials, and it is quicker when cutting and composing than other Cricut models. With everything incorporated that makes Cricut so mainstream, and substantially more, in addition, this is the most expandable machine in the arrangement. Encased here, you'll discover ground-breaking cutting edges, a scoring tool, and pens.

The turning sharp edge right now to slice through practically any texture quickly, with the blade edge additionally downplaying most errands, all on the two cutting mats notwithstanding. This model has a stunning 50 prepared to-make designs which are without altogether, just as 25 sewing designs. Using this machine couldn't be simpler as you simply browse the basic plan application, spread it out on your gadget, and the Cricut denotes every one of the pieces for you. Finding a good pace cutting, it's ideal for the two fledglings, as your first project materials are included, and experts, as it is an incredible Cricut machine for educators or the individuals who achieve various projects, because of its usability and cutting pace. You can even utilize your own structures in the event that you'd like.

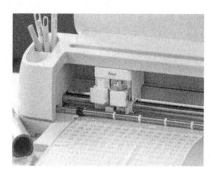

This machine has the ability to hold your cell phone or tablet, permitting you to charge such gadgets through its USB port or interface remotely through its Bluetooth innovation.

Clients of the Cricut Maker profoundly rate its usability. However, it's the capacity to offer unlimited potential outcomes when slicing through even the hardest of materials, yet still with accurate results.

Pros

• Endless projects conceivable

• Wireless

- Writes and scores

- Tool holder

- Good for educators/experts

- Unique frill accessible

Cons

• Expensive model on the rundown

Cricut Explore Air 2.

Highlights

• Size: up to 12 x 24 inches

• Workable materials: 100+, including fundamental and strength Vinyl hues, Iron-on Vinyls, Cardstock, Faux Leather and then some

• Writing: yes

• Scoring: yes

• Wireless: yes

Pros

•   Bluetooth inserted

•   Two times quicker than standard Cricut machines

•   Tool holder

•   Smart set dial

•   Premium fine sharp edge included

Cons

• Many reports of programming and web association issues expressed.

3. Cricut Explore Air – Best Wireless Machine

Highlights

• Size: up to 24 x 12 inches

• Materials: 100, including cardstock, vinyl, and iron-on, just as forte materials

• Writing: yes

• Scoring: yes

• Wireless: yes

Pros

•   Compatibility with all Cricut cartridges

- Cut savvy accuracy

- Smart set dial

- 50,000 available pictures

- Storage compartments

- Embedded Bluetooth

- Fine point cutting edge tool included.

Cons

• Software issues expressed

• Some guarantee not extraordinary for amateurs.

4. The Cricut Explore 1 – Best for Custom Designs

Highlights

• Size: up to 24 x 12 inches

• Materials: Different100 materials, including cardstock, vinyl, and iron-on

• Writing: yes

• Scoring: yes

• Wireless: no

More highlights: Fine-Point Blade for cutting a wide assortment of materials; good with Scoring Stylus, Deep-Point Blade, and different tools. The Cricut Explore One gets our decision in favor of the best Cricut machine for special crafts. On the off chance that you like to cut remotely utilizing all way of gadgets, this machine permits you to with the straightforward utilization of a Bluetooth connector, in this way, overhauling immediately. This guarantees interminable plausibility from those cloud-based free applications for refreshed telephones, MACS, and PCs. Including a brilliant set dial for common material settings, here you can cut tremendous measures of changed material without wasting time with muddled settings! On the other hand, in the event that you'd like to make and make the settings for a particular material, here you can. From the standard paper to vinyl iron-on, this machine can without much of a stretch adapt to even those thicker of materials, for example, felt and cowhide. Browse the 50,000 or more contributions in the picture library or transfer your own photographs and pictures for nothing.

With most projects finished in minutes, no project is hard to amass on the Cricut Explore One. This model flaunts cut savvy innovation, which means you can cut all way of shapes with the most unpredictable of exactness in sizes. Permitting you to cut and compose or cut and score in only one stage, this model comes total with a top-notch fine point edge, a cutting mat, an example, and even USB ports and fueled ropes. Working with all Cricut cartridges too, this Cricut machine likewise has a helpful opening on one side, permitting you to rest your tools and pens in securely when not being used. Users of the Cricut Explore One locate this very easy to use, close by offering various conceivable outcomes through its remote connector limit. Its speed when playing out an undertaking is profoundly evaluated all through.

Pros

• Smart set dial

• Can be gotten to through applications and the cloud

• Easy settings

• 50,000 pictures in the library

• Tool opening

Cons

• Lack of tools provided

• Software issues

• Requires web to run programs

5. Cricut Cuttlebug – Budget Pick

Highlights

• Size: up to 5 x 12 inches

• Workable materials: tissue paper, foils, acetic acid derivation strip, and dainty cowhide, and that's only the tip of the iceberg

• Writing: no

• Scoring: no

• Wireless: no

More highlights: cuts and decorates an assortment of materials

The Cricut Cuttlebug is the Budget pick and maybe the best Cricut machine for apprentices. A most minimal structure, it flaunts everything that you have to begin. This comes total with an A Plate and two B plates and an elastic embellishing mat. As a little something extra, you'll additionally discover an A2 emblazoning envelope, and two metal bites the dust.

This model is perfect for getting together and taking out in a hurry; such is its compactable overlay and store plan – just as its collapsible handle includes. Despite the fact that it might be little in stature, it can look at a present slice through a wide assortment of materials – from foil and tissue paper to acetic acid derivation strip and even meager calfskin.

CHAPTER 2:

Setting Up Step By Step

1. Opening the Box

When you purchase a bundle from Cricut, you will receive a few boxes, but the most significant box amongst them will hold the Cricut Maker. To recognize it, you'll see the picture of the Maker on the box.

When opening the Cricut box, the first thing you see is the welcome packet placed on the machine. The welcome package contains a welcome manuscript, a rotary blade with cover, a fine point pen, a USB cable, and a packet with your first project.

When you take the Cricut machine out of the box, the power cord will be underneath along with the cutting mats. You will also see half of the settings on the dial between the fabrics. This is for when you need a little less or a little more force than is given by the programmed settings. If you cut a light cardstock, for example, but the knife doesn't completely cut the design, you can pick the half setting between Light and Cardstock. Or if you cut a poster board and the blade exerts too much pressure by slicing your pad, simply select the arrangement between the cloth and the poster board. If you use another product and face it, you can use this tool well over a hundred different materials so why wouldn't you? All what you need to do is just to change the dial to the setting' Custom.' You can then pick the exact product you are using from the massive drop-down list in Design Space. And again, the Cricut changes its blade settings automatically so that you don't have to.

2. Unwrapping

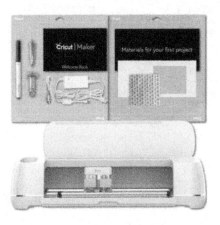

The Cricut machine is wrapped with a layer of cellophane and a protective wrapper. Before setting up the device, you have to remove the wrappings.

Some Styrofoam protects the in-housing of the machine, and that has to go too.

Your Cricut Maker will also come with some supplies, and you should unwrap them and check them out. Lucky for you, the fine point blade is already installed in the Cricut Maker, so you don't have to bother with that.

3. Visit cricut.com/setup

The following step in setting up your machine lies in the technical aspects. Cricut has a webpage dedicated to walking you through this process, which makes it super easy.

Open cricut.com/setup on your device. You can use any device that is compatible with Cricut like a smartphone, tablet or computer. When you do that, you will be asked to install Cricut Design Space and also sign up. Then, you'll be given your Cricut ID.

If you have been using a former Cricut machine before, then you can carry on with your former ID.

4. Plugging It In

Then, you need to take your USB cord and the power cord to power up your Cricut machine.

This will be shown on the setup wizard of the webpage.

For the USB cord, you connect the square end to the Cricut Maker device and the other end to the computer. And, the power cord is easy to connect the Cricut Maker to the power outlet.

5. Claim Your Bonus

After plugging in your Cricut, you will be able to claim a free welcome bonus from Cricut, which is a free month of Cricut Access. This means that you get to enjoy access to projects, fonts, and Cricut Cut Files.

6. Begin Your Project

If you need a little something to practice with before starting on your intended project, Cricut Maker machines usually come with a little project in the welcome pack to help you get acquainted with the tools.

The Maker comes with all the tools that you need to complete the project, which is usually the task of making a little card.

After this, then you can begin using it. The thing is, when you want to use your Cricut Maker, you need to learn how to use Cricut Design Space.

CHAPTER 3:

Cricut Tools and Accessory

Cricut Explore Cutting Blades

Both Cricut Explore Machines come with an extremely sharp German carbide fine-point blade. This allows all users to get started cutting right away. It comes already housed within the Cricut machine and is easily removable and sharpened in the event that the blade gets dull. A user tip on keeping your blade sharp and long-lasting is to stick the blade into a ball... This allows you to continue using the same blade for an extended period of time, and saving you money as well! A fine-point cutting blade is typically used for almost all of the Cricut design cutting projects, and will last through many projects when taken care of properly. If you are continually cutting rough materials, it is recommended to sharpen the blade often. The housing for this blade is silver on the older style machines and has been upgraded to gold for the new generation of machines.

The following type of blade that is commonly used is the Deep Cut blade. This is the type of blade you will need in order to cut thicker materials. These materials include thin wood and leather. You heard that right; you can cut leather with a Cricut machine! With this blade, you will need to get its custom housing piece, which you can purchase separately. When using this blade, you will simply need to swap out the housing pieces and then attach the blade as necessary. Similarly, as the fine-point blade, you will need to take care of this blade and sharpen it often. Since you are using thick materials for this blade, you may have to replace it more often if using it all the time. The housing for this type of cut blade is black. You also will have the option to purchase cut blades individually once you have the housing unit.

Cricut Maker Cutting Blades

In addition to the Explore Cutting blade, the Cricut Maker has additional cutting blades that allow for intricate cutting details on a variety of materials.

The Cricut Maker comes with one additional blade, the revolutionary rotary cutting blade for use on cutting all sorts of fabrics. Unlike the average rotary blade, this one lasts far longer because it avoids the nicks that typically come with its line of duty. You can buy additional blades individually, but one blade should last throughout multiple projects.

Cutting Mats

Cricut cutting mats come in a variety of sizes and degree of stickiness. Depending on what material you are using, you will want less or more stickiness on your mat.

Standard grip Mats can be used for most of your project cutting needs. You are able to cut cardstock, vinyl, and iron-on, etc. with this mat.

There is also a Pink Fabric cutting mat, something that is necessary when cutting any time of fabric with a Cricut Maker machine. It comes in a 12"x12" size or a 12"x24" size, depending on how large your project cut is.

The Circuit Weeder

The weeder tool, which looks similar to a dental pick, is used for removing negative space from a vinyl project. This weeder tool is a must when doing any type of project that involves vinyl. Trying to get rid of access vinyl is nearly impossible without a weeder especially with materials like glitter iron-on. A weeder is a useful tool for any type of project using adhesives. Instead of picking up the adhesive with your fingertips, user the weeder tool and keep your fingers sticky mess free!

The Cricut Scraper

The Circuit Scraper tool is essential (and a lifesaver!) when you need to rid your cutting mat of excess negative bits. This tool typically works best with paper, such as cardstock, but other materials can easily be scraped up as well. Use the flexibility of the mat to your advantage as you scrap the bits off the mat, to ensure you are not scraping up the adhesive on the mat as well. You can also use the Cricut Scraper as a score line holder, which allows you to fold over the scoreline with a nice crisp edge. It can also be used as a burnishing tool for Cricut transfer tape, as it will allow seamless separation of the transfer tape from the backing.

The Cricut Spatula

A spatula is a must-have tool for a crafter who works with a lot of paper. Pulling the paper off of a Cricut cut mat can result in a lot of tearing and paper curling if you are not diligent and mindful when you are removing it. The spatula is thinly designed to slip right under paper which allows you to ease it off the mat carefully. Be sure to clean it often as it is likely to get the adhesive build up on it after multiple uses.

The Cricut Tweezers

Projects that involve a lot of embellishments will require a pair of tweezers. The Cricut tweezers can be a bit awkward to use at first, as they function directly opposite than we are used to with traditional tweezers. They need to be squeezed to open them, as opposed to squeezing them to shut. Ultimately you will begin to realize the genius behind this design because you will be able to pick something up and release pressure on it as the Cricut tweezers will hold pressure on the object. You'll save yourself from continuously dropping small pieces, and many hand cramps!

The Cricut Scissors

Using the right scissors for a job can make a world of difference. The Cricut Scissors are made from stainless steel to ensure they will stick around for many jobs before getting dull. The scissors come with a micro-tip blade, so finer details in smaller areas are easier and clean right down to a point.

The Cricut Scoring Tool

If you want to do projects that involve a scoring line, such as folding cards in half or making 3D boxes, you will want to invest in a Cricut Scoring tool. You can insert this tool into the second tool holder, or accessory clamp, into the Cricut Explore itself, and the Cricut will use it to make score lines wherever the design dictates. They will need to be present in the Cricut Design Space file in order for the machine to recognize the scoreline is needed in the project. The basic tool kit sold by Cricut does not come with a scoring tool you will need to purchase this separately. If you plan to work with a lot of paper projects, this is a worthy tool to invest in.

The Cricut Easy press

If you begin to venture into iron-on projects and want to upgrade from a traditional iron and ironing board, the Cricut Easypress is the right way to go. It will make projects so much easier than using a traditional iron. The Cricut Easypress is known to help keep designed adhered for longer, essentially no more peeling of designs after one or two uses and washes. The Easypress also takes all of the guesswork out of the right amount of contact time as well as temperature. You will not run the peril of burning your transfer paper or fabric!

The Cricut Brightpad

Brightpad reduces eyestrain while making crafting easier. It is designed to illuminate fine lines for tracing, cut lines for weeding and so much more! It is thin and lightweight which allows for durable transportation. The only downfall to this accessory is that it must be plugged in while it is used. It does not contain a rechargeable battery.

The Cricut Cuttlebug Machine

The Cricut Cuttlebug is embossing and dies cutting machine that offers portability and versatility when it comes to cutting and embossing. This machine gives professional looking results with clean, crisp, and deep embosses. This machine goes beyond paper, allowing you to emboss tissue paper, foils, thin leather, and more!

We sincerely hope this unit gives you a better understanding of the tools and accessories that can be used with the Cricut cutting machines and how best to put them into use when designing and creating your own projects! Know that these tools are here to make your life easier it's worth investing in them!

CHAPTER 4:

Cricut Mats

Cricut cutting mat is where the cutting takes place. You have to clean and maintain your cricut cutting mat. If the cutting mat isn't clean, it can stain the machine. Also, if your cutting mat has stopped sticking, it can spoil your designs and creations.

When your mat is no longer sticky because of debris and grime, cleaning it and making it sticky again will bring it back to life.

The solutions that I will mention are not ideal for the pink cutting mats, only for the green, blue, and purple.

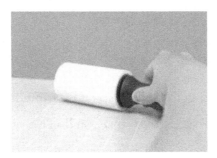

There are many ways to clean your cutting mat.

- Using baby wipes:

Make use of alcohol-free, unscented, and bleach-free baby wipes to clean your mat. You should use the plainest baby wipes that you can find so that you don't add lotions, cornstarch, solvents or oils to your cutting mat. If not, you could affect the stickiness and adhesive of the mat. Also, after cleaning it let it dry completely before using it.

- Using a Sticky Lint Roller

You can also use a roll of masking tape if you don't find a sticky lint roller. Run the roll across the mat to get rid of hairs, fibers, specks of dust, and paper particles.

This form of cleaning can be done daily or between projects so that dust doesn't accumulate on the mat. This is a fast way to remove dirt apart from using tweezers or scrapers.

- Using warm water with soap

You can also clean the mat with soap and warm water. You should use the plainest soap possible too so that you don't mess with the mat. Use a clean cloth, sponge, soft brush, or a magic eraser. Also, rinse it thoroughly and don't use it until it is completely dry.

- Using an adhesive remover

In the case of heavy-duty cleaning, then you should use a reliable adhesive remover to clean it properly. When using an adhesive remover, read the directions properly before you start.

Then, spray a little amount on the mat and spread it around with a scraper or anything that can act as a makeshift scraper.

Wait for a few minutes so that the solvent can work on the mat. Then, scrape the dirty adhesive off your mat with a scraper, paper towels, or cloth.

After this, wash the mat with warm water and soap in case there is leftover residue and let it dry properly.

How to Make Your Cutting Mat Sticky Again

After washing or cleaning your cutting mat, you have to make them sticky again.

The most advisable way to make your mat sticky again is by adding glue to it. Get a solid glue stick like the Zig 2-Way Glue Pen and apply it on the inner portion of the mat. Then, stroke the glue around the mat and ensure that there is no glue residue on the edges of the mat.

After about 30 minutes, the glue will turn clear. If the cutting mat turns out to be too sticky after you apply glue, you can use a piece of fabric to reduce the adhesive by pressing the material on the parts of the mat that are very sticky.

Cover the mat with a clear film cover after a few hours.

You can also use tacky glues or spray adhesives that are ideal for cutting mats.

General Maintenance

When your mat isn't in use, cover it with a clear film cover so that dust and hairs won't accumulate on the surface of the mat.

Handle your mats with care. If you want to ensure that the adhesive does not get damaged, avoid touching the sticky surface with your hands.

Always ensure that your mat dries entirely before using it or covering it up. Don't use heat when drying your mat, but you can place it in front of a fan. Also, ensure that it is drying hanging up so that both sides will dry.

CHAPTER 5:

Cricut Projects

Wedding Invitation

Materials needed – "Cricut" cutting machine, cutting mat, and cardstock or your choice of decorative paper/crepe paper/fabric, home printer (if not using "Cricut Maker").

Step 1

Use your "Cricut ID" to log in to the "Design Space" application. Then click on the "New Project" button on the top right corner of the screen to start a new project and view a blank canvas.

Step 2

A beginner-friendly way to create wedding invitations is a customization of an already existing project form the "Design Space" library that aligns with your own ideas. Click on the "Projects" icon on the "Design Panel" then select "Cards" from the "All Categories" drop-down. Enter the keywords "wedding invite" in the search bar.

Step 3

You can click on the project to preview its description and requirements. Once you have found the project you want to use, click "Customize" at the bottom of the screen, so you can edit the invite and add the required text to it.

Step 4

The design will be loaded on to the canvas. Click on the "Text" button and type in the details for your invite. You will be able to modify the font, color as well as the alignment of the text from the "Edit Text Bar" on top of the screen. You can even adjust the size of the entire design as needed. (An invitation card can be anywhere from 6 to 9 inches wide)

Note – Most cards will require you to change the "Fill" to "Print" on the top of the screen so you can first print then cut the invitation.

Step 5

Select the entire design and click on the "Group" icon on the top right of the screen under "Layers Panel." Then click on the "Save" button to enter a name for your project and click "Save" again.

Step 6

Your design can now be printed then cut. Simply click on the "Make It" button on the top right corner of the screen to view the required mats and material. Then use your home printer to print the design on your chosen material (white cardstock or paper), or if using the "Cricut Maker," then just follow the prompts on the "Design Space" application.

Tip – Calibrate your machine first for the "Print then Cut" project by clicking on the hamburger icon following to the "Canvas" on the top left of the screen and follow the prompts on the screen, as shown in the picture below.

Step 7

Load the material with printed design to your "Cricut" cutting machine and click "Continue" at the bottom right corner of the screen to start cutting your design.

Note – If images and/or fonts used for your design are not free and available for purchase only, then the "Continue" button will not appear, and instead, a "Purchase" button will be visible. Once you have paid for the image or font, the "Continue" button will be available to you.

Step 8

Once you're "Cricut" device has been connected to your computer, set the cut setting to "cardstock." Then place the printed cardstock on top of the cutting mat and load into the "Cricut" device by pushing against the rollers. The "Load/Unload" button would already be flashing, so just press that button first, followed by the flashing "Go" button. Viola! You have your wedding invitations all ready to be put in an envelope and on their way to all your wedding guests.

Paper Lollipop

Materials needed – "Cricut" cutting machine, light grip mat, patterned cardstock in desired colors, glitter, wooden dowels, and hot glue.

Step 1

Use your "Cricut ID" to log in to the "Design Space" application. Then click on the "New Project" button on the top right corner of the screen to start a new project and view a blank canvas.

Step 2

We will be using an already existing project from the "Cricut" library and customizing it. So click on the "Projects" icon and type in "paper lollipop" in the search bar.

Step 3

Click on "Customize" so you can further edit this project to your preference.

Step 4

Once you have altered the design to your satisfaction, it is ready to be cut. Simply click on the "Make It" button on the top right corner of the screen to view the required mats and material for your project.

Step 5

Load the cardstock to your "Cricut" cutting machine and click "Continue" at the bottom right corner of the screen to start cutting your design.

Note – If images and/or fonts used for your design are not free and available for purchase only, then the "Continue" button will not appear, and instead, a "Purchase" button will be visible. Once you have paid for the image or font, the "Continue" button will be available to you.

Step 6

Connect your "Cricut" device to your computer and place the cardstock on top of the cutting mat and load it into the "Cricut" machine by pushing against the rollers. The "Load/Unload" button would already be flashing, so just press that button first, followed by the flashing "Go" button.

Step 7

Use the hot glue to adhere the wooden dowels between the lollipop circles. Then brush the tops with the craft glue and sprinkle on the glitter, as shown in the picture below.

Paper Flowers

Materials needed – "Cricut" cutting machine, cutting mat, cardstock, and adhesive.

Step 1

Use your "Cricut ID" to log in to the "Design Space" application. Then click on the "New Project" button on the top right corner of the screen to start a new project and view a blank canvas.

Step 2

Click on the "Images" icon on the "Design Panel" and type in "flower" in the search bar. Then select the image that you like and click on the "Insert Images" button at the bottom of the screen.

Step 3

The selected image will be showed on the canvas and can be edited using related tools from the "Edit Image Bar." Then copy and paste the flower five times and make them a size smaller than the preceding flower to create a variable size for depth and texture for the design. Click on the "Linetype Swatch" to view the color palette and select the desired color for your design.

Step 5

Once you have adjusted the design to your gratification, it is ready to be cut. Simply click on the "Make It" button on the top right corner of the screen to view the required mats and material for your project.

Step 6

Load the cardstock to your "Cricut" cutting machine and click "Continue" at the bottom right corner of the screen to start cutting your design.

Note – If images and/or fonts used for your design are not free and available for purchase only, then the "Continue" button will not appear, and instead, a "Purchase" button will be visible. Once you have paid for the image or font, the "Continue" button will be available to you.

Step 7

Connect your "Cricut" device to your computer and place the cardstock or your chosen paper on top of the cutting mat and load into the "Cricut" machine by pushing against the rollers. The "Load/Unload" button would already be flashing, so just press that button first, followed by the flashing "Go" button.

Step 8

Once the design has been cut, simply remove the cut flowers and bend them at the center. Then using the adhesive, stack the flowers with the largest flower at the bottom.

Ornaments

These paper adornments can be tweaked in various manners. An essential thought is to choose the number of layers you'd prefer to utilize. In my model, I utilized 5 layers. However, you can attempt three or even 6... Play with the hope to see which you like best.

Materials

• Cricut Machine and Cricut Design Space

• Ornament SVG cut document.

• White cardstock

• Glue

• Twine

Cut lovely plans with your Cricut

Guidelines

1. Upload the trimming cut record to Cricut Design Space.

2. Ungroup and resize the beautiful layer you'd prefer to utilize. Make a point to set the scoreline to SCORE in Design Space.

3. Send the structure to the tangle. Alter the cut amount to cut 5 duplicates of the structure. Organize on the tangle anyway you'd like.

4. Fold each cut structure along the scoreline.

5. Apply the paste to the other side of a cut shape. Line up the subsequent cut shape, press and hold set up to follow together.

6. Repeat until you've applied all the cut shapes into a solitary 3D decoration.

7. Applying the twine: You have two alternatives for applying twine to your trimming.

1.   You can basically wrap and tie the twine around the highest point of the trimming at the neck of the ball shape.

2.   You can add a length of twine to the focal point of your adornment before sticking the last different sides together. In the event that you pick this strategy, try to make a bunch at the top and base of the twine, so the twine doesn't sneak out of the focal point of the decoration.

Greeting Cards

Many people buy their first Cricut Maker with the idea of making greeting cards. If you look on Etsy, you will see dozens of people selling home-made cards and earning extra money using their Cricut Maker to make these cards. Many users recommend a Cricut Access Membership. This will give you access to thousands of images, hundreds of fonts and discounts off purchases for supplies and accessories.

CHAPTER 6:

Make Money with Cricut

I t is a well-known fact in the world of business that to make money, you first need to invest money. With that being said, if you already own a "Cricut" cutting machine, then you can jump to the following paragraph, but if you are debating if it's worth the investment, then read on. As mentioned earlier, "Cricut" has a range of cutting machines with distinctive capabilities offered at a varying price range. Now, if you were to buy any of these machines during a holiday sale with a bundle deal that comes with a variety of tools, accessories, and materials for a practice project as well as free trial membership to "Cricut Access", you would already be saving enough to justify the purchase for your personal usage. The cherry on top would be if you can use this investment to make more money. You can always get additional supplies in a bundle deal or from your local stores at a much cheaper price. All in all, those upfront costs can easily be justified with the expenses you budget for school projects that require you to cut letters and shapes, creating personalized gifts for your loved ones or decorating your home with customized decals, and of course, your own jewelry creations. These are only a handful of the reasons to buy a "Cricut" machine for your personal use. Let's start scraping the mountain of "Cricut" created wealth to help you get rich while enjoying your work!

At this stage, let's assume that you have bought a "Cricut" cutting machine and have enough practice with the beginner-friendly projects described earlier in this manuscript. You now have the skillset and the tools to start making money with your "Cricut" machine, so let's jump into how you can make it happen. The ways listed below have been tried and tested as successful money-making strategies that you can implement with no hesitations.

Selling pre-cut customized vinyl

Vinyl is super beginner friendly material to work with and comes in a variety of colors and patterns to add to its great reputation. You can create customized labels for glass containers and canisters to help anyone looking to organize their pantry. Explore the online trends and adjust the labels. Once you have your labels designed, the easiest approach is to set up an "Etsy" shop, which is free and very easy to use. It's almost like opening an Amazon prime membership account. If your design is in demand, you will have people ordering even with no advertising. But if you would like to keep the tempo high, then advertise your "Etsy" listing on "Pinterest" and other social media platforms. This is a sure-shot way to generate more traffic to your "Etsy" shop and turning potential customers into paying customers. An important note here is the pictures being used on your listing. You cannot use any of the stock images from the "Design Space" application and must use your own pictures that match the product you are selling.

Create a package of 5 or 6 different labels like sugar, salt, rice, oats, beans, etc. that can be sold as a standard packager and offer a customized package that will allow the customer to request any word that they need to be included in their set. Since these labels weigh following to nothing, shipping can easily be managed with standard mail with usually only a single postage stamp, depending on the delivery address. Make sure you do not claim the following day or two-day delivery for these. Build enough delivery time so you can create and ship the labels without any stress. Once you have an established business model, you can adjust the price and shipping of your product, but more on that far along. Check out other "Etsy" listings to make sure your product pricing is competitive enough, and you are attracting enough potential buyers.

Now, once you have traction in the market, you can offer additional vinyl-based projects like bumper stickers, iron-on, or heat transfer vinyl designs that people can transfer on their clothing using a standard heating iron. Really, once you have gained some clientele, you can modify and customize all your listings to develop into a one-stop-shop for all things vinyl (great name for your future Etsy shop, right!).

Selling finished pieces

You would be using your "Cricut" machines for a variety of personal projects like home décor, holiday décor, personalized clothing, and more. Following time you embark on another one of your creative journeys leading to unique creations, just make two of everything, and you can easily put the other product to sell on your "Etsy" shop. Another great advantage is that you will be able to save all your projects on the "Design Space" application for future use so if one of your projects goes viral, you can easily buy the supplies and turn them into money-making offerings. This way, not only your original idea for personal usage will be paid off, but you can make much more money than you invested in it, to begin with.

Again, spend some time researching what kind of designs and decorations are trending in the market and use them to spark up inspiration for your following project. Some of the current market trends include customized cake and cupcake toppers and watercolor designs that can be framed as fancy wall decorations. The cake toppers can be made with cardstock, which is another beginner-friendly material, light in weight, and can be economically shipped tucked inside an envelope.

Personalized Clothing and Accessories

T-shirts with cool designs and phrases are all the rage right now. Just follow a similar approach to the selling vinyl unit and take it up a notch. You can create sample clothing with iron-on design and market it with "can be customized further at no extra charge" or "transfer the design on your own clothing" to get traction in the market. You can buy sling bags and customize them with unique designs to be sold as finished products at a higher price than a plain boring sling bag.

Consider creating a line of products with a centralized theme like the DC Marvel characters or the "Harry Potter" movies and design custom t-shirts, hats, and even bodysuits for babies. You can create customized party favor boxes and gift bags at the request of the customer. Once your product has a dedicated customer base, you can get project ideas from them directly and quote them a price for your work. Isn't that great?!?!

Another big advantage of the heat transfer vinyl, as mentioned earlier, is that anyone can transfer the design on their desired item of clothing using a standard household iron. But you would need to include the transfer instructions with the order letting them know exactly how to prep for the heat transfer without damaging their chosen clothing item. And again, heat transfer vinyl can be easily shipped using a standard mailing envelope. We have added a dedicated unit on tips for using everyday iron-on with a household iron.

Marketing on Social Media

We are all aware of how social media has become a marketing platform for not only established corporations, but also small businesses and budding entrepreneurs. Simply add hashtags like for sale, product, selling, free shipping, sample included, and more to entice potential buyers. Join "Facebook" community pages and groups for handcraft sellers and buyers to market your products. Use catchy phrases like customization available at no extra cost or free returns if not satisfied when posting the products on these pages as well as your personal "Facebook" page. Use "Twitter" to share feedback from your satisfied customers to widen your customer base. You can do this by creating a satisfaction survey that you can email to your buyers or include a link to your "Etsy" listing asking for online appraisals and ratings from your customers.

Another tip here is to post pictures of anything and everything you have created using "Cricut" machines, even those that you did not plan to sell. You never know who else might need something that you deemed unsellable. Since you will be creating these only after the order has been placed, you can easily gather the required supplies after the fact and get crafting.

Target local farmer's market and boutiques

If you like the thrill of a show-and-tell, then reserve a booth at a local farmer's market and show up with some ready to sell crafts. In this case, you are relying on the number of people attending and a subset of those who might be interested in making a purchase from you. If you are in an urban neighborhood where people are keenly interested in unique art designs but do not have the time to create them on their own, you can easily make big bucks by setting a decent price point for your products.

Bring flyers to hand out people so they can reach you through one of your social media accounts or email and check all your existing "Etsy" listings. Think of these events as a means of marketing for those who are not as active online but can be excited with customized products to meet their following big life event like baby shower, birthday party, or a wedding.

One downside to participating in local events is the generation of mass inventory and booth displays, topped with expenses to load and transport the inventory. You may or may not be able to sell all of the inventory depending on the size of the event, but as I said earlier, you can still make the most of this by marketing your products and building up a local clientele.

CHAPTER 7:

Maintaining the Cricut Machine

I f you want your Cricut Machine to last for a very long time, you have to maintain it routinely. This means cleaning it properly and also maintaining the cutting mats and blades.

When using your Cricut machine, over time, it will inevitably collect paper particles, dust, and debris. Also, grease in the device will begin to stick to the carriage track.

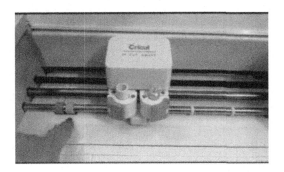

If you want your machine to last long, then you should clean it regularly, or else it can get damaged prematurely. Here are some cleaning tips to help you out when cleaning the machine.

- Before cleaning your machine, disconnect it from the power outlet. This will prevent electrocution or any other accident that can damage the device or injure you.

- When cleaning your machine, don't use any form of acetone. Acetone, like nail polish remover, will damage the plastic parts of the device permanently.

- You can clean the machine using a glass cleaner instead. Spray it on a clean, soft cloth and wipe the device gently.

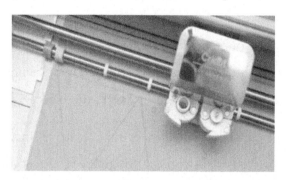

- In the case of grease buildup on the carriage tracks, then you should use a tissue, cotton swab, or a soft, clean cloth to wipe it off gently.

- There is also the case of a buildup of static electricity on your machine. This can cause dust, debris, and particles to form on the device. This can also be easily cleaned with a soft, clean cloth.

Application of Grease for the Cricut Explore Models

- Disconnect the Cricut machine from the power outlet.

- Push the Cut Smart carriage gently to the left.

- Wipe the entire Cut Smart carriage bar with a tissue. The bar is the surface in front of the belt where the carriage slides on.

- Push the Cut Smart carriage gently to the right.

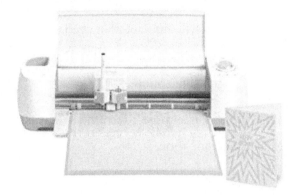

- Repeat the cleaning process for the other side by cleaning the bar with clean tissue.

- Then, push the Cut Smart carriage to the center of the bar.

- Take a lubrication packet, open it, and squeeze out a little grease. Put the amount of grease on a clean cotton swab.

- Apply a small coating of the grease on the two sides of the Cut Smart carriage around the bar so that it will form a quarter inches ring on both sides.

- In order to make the grease become even in the carriage, push the Cut Smart carriage to the both sides slowly and repeatedly.

- Clean off any grease that stained the bar while you were greasing the machine.

- You can purchase a grease packet from Cricut. This will work better than using a third-party grease packet so that the machine will not get damaged. This is especially if, after using another grease product, your Cricut machine is making a grinding sound.

- This process is almost the same as greasing your Cricut Maker machine too.

Cleaning and Care

Cleaning your machine is very important, and you should do it regularly to keep everything in tip-top shape. If you don't take care of your machine, that's just money down the drain.

But what can you do to care for your machine? Well, I do suggest initially that you make sure to run maintenance on it as much as you can and keep it clean. There are a few other tips and tricks that can help prolong the machine's life. For starters, keep liquids and food away from the machine – never drink or eat while you use your Cricut machine. Set up your machine in a location that's free of dust and try to keep it away from excessive coolness or heat, so don't just throw it in the attic or an especially cold basement. If you're transporting your machine to use it at a different location, never leave it in the car. Excessive heat will melt the machine's plastic components, so be careful.

Finally, make sure the machine is stored away from sunlight. Keep it out of places in the home where sunlight hits it directly. For example, if you have an office that is very bright and the sun warms the machine for a long period of time, you'll want to move it so that it doesn't get damaged.

Be gentle with your machine. Remember, it is a machine, so you'll want to make sure that you do take some time and try to keep it nice and in order. Don't be rough with it, and when working with the machine parts, don't be too rough with them, either.

Caring for your machine isn't just about making sure that the parts don't get dirty, but you should also make sure that you keep everything in good working order.

Cleaning the Machine Itself

In general, the exterior is pretty easy to clean – you just need a damp cloth. Use a soft cloth to wipe it off, and keep in mind that chemical cleaners with benzene, acetone, or carbon tetrachloride should never be used on your Cricut machine. Any cleaner that is scratchy, as well, should be avoided at all costs.

Make sure that you never put any machine components in water. This should be obvious, but often, people may use a piece of a damp cloth, thinking that it'll be fine when in reality, it isn't.

You should consider getting some non-alcoholic wipes for cleaning your machine. Always disconnect the power before cleaning, as you would with any machine. The Cricut machine can then be lightly wiped down. Some people also use a glass cleaner sprayed on a cloth but do be careful to make sure no residue builds up. If you notice there is some dust there, you can typically get away with a cloth that's soft and clean.

Sometimes, grease can build up – you may notice this on the cartridge bar if you use cartridges a lot. Use a swab of cotton or a soft cloth to remove it.

Greasing the Machine

If you need to grease your machine, first make sure that it's turned off and the smart carriage is moved to the left. Use a tissue to wipe this down, and then move it to the right, repeating the process again.

From there, move the carriage to the center and open up a lubrication package. Put a small amount onto a Q-tip. Apply a thin coating, greasing everything evenly, and also clean any buildup that may have occurred. This is usually the issue if you hear grinding noise when cleaning the machine itself.

There are a few other important places that you should make sure to clean, besides the outside and the carriage. Any places where blades are should be cleaned; you can just move the housing unit of the blade to clean it. You should also check the drawing area, to make sure there isn't any excessive ink there.

Never use spray cleaner directly on the machine, for obvious reasons. The bar holding the housing shouldn't be wiped down, but if you do notice an excessive grease, please take the time to make sure that it's cleaned up. Remember to never touch the gear chain near the back of this unit, either, and never clean with the machine on, for your own safety.

When caring for a Cricut machine, try to do this more frequently if you're using the machine a lot, or twice yearly. If you notice strange noises coming from the machine, do get a grease packet. You can always contact Cricut and they'll help you figure out the issue, if there is one, with your machine.

Cricut machines are great, but you need to take care in making sure that you keep everything in rightful order.

Cutting Blade

Your blades will tend to dull over time, but this is usually a very slow process. The best way to prevent it is to have different blades to cut different materials. Having a different blade for each material is a really good idea.

You can get fine-point ones which are good for smaller items; deep-cut, which is great for leather and other fabrics; bonded fabric, so great for fabric pieces; a rotary blade for those heavy fabrics; and finally, a knife blade, which is good for those really thick items.

In order to maintain your blades, you should clean the housing area for every blade after each use, since they get gunky fast. Squirting compressed air into the area is a wonderful way to get the dust out of there.

As for the blades, remember foil? Use a little bit of that over the edges of the blade to help clean and polish them up. To polish them, you should put them on the cutting mat and from there, cut small designs on it. It actually does help with sharpening them, and it doesn't require you to remove them completely. You can do this with every single blade, too!

To change the blades in their housings, just open the clamps, pull up, and remove the housing within the machine. Put a new blade in, and then close it. That's all it takes.

Storing them is also pretty simple. There is a drop-down doorway at the front area of the machine. It's made for storing the blades within their housings. Put your loose blades in there first, and then utilize the magnet to keep them in place. The best part about this storage is that your blades are always with the Cricut, even if you take the machine somewhere else.

There is also a blade organizer that you can use, too, made out of chipboard with some holders attached. This is also a wonderful means to store all of your items. Organizing your Cricut blades is very important, and understanding the best places to keep them is, of course, essential.

CHAPTER 8:

Beginner Project Ideas

Have you ever wondered how custom T-shirts are made? Well, you are not the only one, as most of us are suckers for such apparel. If you want to make some T-shirts for yourself, then I have great news for you: they are quite easy to make using the right technology on your Cricut Machine. You heard me right! These T-shirts can be created using one of the most common and basic Cricut materials: iron-on vinyl. The process can also be called heat transfer vinyl (aka HTV).

This is the perfect choice to have on your T-shirts, or on adorable baby bodysuits. So, let's start with your requirements. For this project you will need:

- Cricut Explore (any model) or Cricut Maker

- Cricut Iron-On Vinyl

- Bodysuit or a T-shirt

- Green Standard Grip mat or a Blue Light Grip mat

- Weeding tool

- Cricut EasyPress, a heat press, or an Iron

- piece of fabric of at least 9" x 9" (but this is optional)

- files from Cricut Access with text and models of your choice

First, you will need to open the Cricut Design Space to use images from the Library, so go to the Design Panel from the left side and click Images. Search for very interesting images that you think would work very nicely with your T-shirt. Once the files are opened in Canvas, you can resize them by using the Edit Toolbar (located at the top). You can choose to increase the size a bit on the images you selected. To avoid any material waste, use the ColorSync panel (from the top left corner of the Layers Panel), to drag and drop images on the same layer, to appear on the same color. If they appear on the same color, they will be cut on the same mat.

When you are satisfied with the end result, click the Make It button from the top side of the Canvas. You will then see the Preview screen, and very important, in this screen you will need to click "Mirror" in the sidebar to flip the image, otherwise the image will be shown backward when you want to iron it. When you see the slider on the left green, and the project showing up backward on the mat, you know that the settings are right. Please click "Continue" and when you get to the Make screen, you will have to connect your Cricut Machine. From the Smart Set Dial (for Explore machines), select Iron-On, if you are using Cricut Maker, select the Iron-On material from the list. The blade you will be using for this cut is the Fine-Point Blade.

Once the cut is done, you can press the arrow key and the Cricut machine will simply release your mat. This is when you need to use the Cricut Weeding tool, as you will need to remove anything that it's not part of your project. First, you will need to dig the tip of your weeding tool into a vinyl piece that is not part of your design and pull it up gently. When you have a good chunk of vinyl that is not supposed to be there, you can also use your fingers, but remember to use the weeding tool for more complicated bits (these include the insides of letters as well). Continue to remove all the bits from the side, until only the image remains. If you flip over the design, you will see that the image is facing the right way. Make sure you double-check your work, as you really don't want anything unwanted after the weeding process.

Then, you will need to adhere to the Cricut Iron-On Vinyl. If you have Cricut Easypress that's great, but bear in mind that you can use a simple iron or heat press. Let's say that you don't have an Easypress device or any heat press. In this case, you can just use a plain iron. Make sure that the basin of the iron is completely empty, as you don't want steam on your Iron-On. Before you place the iron on the T-shirt, do a pre-press with the iron for about 5 seconds. This pre-press will make sure that the iron reaches a very high temperature, there is no steam remaining, plus it can help flatten the onesie and starts adhesion once you add the decal.

When you start the ironing process, it's highly recommended to use a piece of cotton on top of the plastic carrier sheet. You don't want to melt the carrier sheet, so this is why it's better to do it this way. Plus, there will not be any uneven heating. Make sure you press down the iron, hold it down firmly for around 15 to 30 seconds, and then pick it up and move it if the image gets larger than your iron. DON'T SLIDE THE IRON!!!

Let the decal cool as the vinyl adhesive gets more time to set. It looks like if you cold peel vinyl, and you give the vinyl adhesive more time to set, the end result will be simply amazing.

This is when you will need to pull back the plastic carrier sheet from the back of your image. Normally, the vinyl should stick, but if it doesn't, put the plastic carrier back on and apply more heat. Tip: press with your iron at the highest heat (don't forget about the piece of cotton) for at least 10 more seconds, flip your project over, and press the iron again (still using the piece of cotton) for around 15 seconds. Then, you can remove the whole plastic and the vinyl should remain.

You can try this process with different apparel, from T-shirts to baby bodysuits. Don't expect to succeed from your first attempt, as you may need to do this a few times until you get it right. Doing such projects on clothes can be very easy, once you get the hang of it, plus these projects are very practical and popular. You can make plenty of money from such projects, and the best part is that you really don't have to invest too much.

Intermediate Level

The Cricut Machine can be used to create even more intricate projects, the ones that have a more decorative role, but they simply look amazing. For such a difficulty level I would suggest a paper flower decoration in a shadow box. The total time spent on this project should not be more than two or three hours. You will need for it a

Cricut Maker, glue, tweezers, and the StandardGrip Mat. Also, for this project, you will need cardstock in multiple colors, straight pins, buttons, beads, or other baubles, and a shadow box of 9" x 9".

You can use different paper flowers from the Giant Flowers cartridge, but also a set of leaves from the Nature Collections cartridge for this project. By the way, they are completely free with Cricut Access. You can get the flowers and leaves that you want using the Cricut Design Space application. Once you open the files using this software, you can duplicate them, resize them, and make all the necessary tweaks you need for your project. After all, it all depends on you how crowded you want that shadow box to be (if you want the flowers to be closer or farther apart).

Once you are satisfied with the flowers, click on the Make It button, connect your Cricut Maker and send the flowers and leaves for cutting. You will see the previews in Design Space, set the colors and the number of mats you will have to use. Also, you will see how the flowers will be laid out on the mat, and set the cardstock to use with which flower. When you are ready to start cutting, load your first mat into the machine and follow the instructions until you get all the mats cut out.

The following step is to weed out the background paper surrounding the cut out flowers and leaves. For the more delicate bits, you will need to use the tweezers from the weeding tool. The Giant Flowers collection, but also the Leaves collection, comes with an instruction manual, so you will know exactly how to assemble them. Follow these instructions closely. You can choose to use glue, just to make sure that everything stays together as you want.

Lay out the flowers to form a monogram letter, then use some straight pins to attach the flowers and leaves to the backing board of the shadow box (you can use glue if you want to make this project permanent). Then you will need to add buttons, beads, and other baubles to the same backing board. The final step requires you to assemble the backing board into the shadow box frame.

Expert Level

Become a pro in creating your own custom decorations, whether we're talking about Christmas, Halloween, or other seasonal decorations.

Create or use some trapezoid panels with 2.3 wide x 0.76". Although you need 6 panels each, it's better to have 2 extra panels, just in case. On the cutting board, you will need to select a custom setting. Choose Chipboard Heavy 0.7 mm and then press GO. When the first cut is complete, press GO to send it through a second time. When you have all the panels cut, you will need to assemble them together by gluing.

Place all the triangle panels together; keeping them as close as you can to glue them together (you can use a light masking tape to hold them together).

Bring together all these trapezoid pieces so it forms a diamond, and then create the holes for the leather cording. You can paint your diamond as you like, but it's recommended to use white, grey sky, or crystal marine. When the paint is dry you can just add the leather cords. Whether you use glue or some wires with the leather cords, it's up to you. Since this is supposed to be decorative, you can go ahead with the artificial plant, and you don't have to worry about anything else. However, if you are using natural plants, you will need to add a plastic container with soil for the natural plant, but also some small white gravel.

CHAPTER 9:

Tips and Tricks

Extras

I t's good to have extras of everything. I'm talking blades, mats, pens, paper, vinyl, everything. If you are buying by the project, make sure you don't buy just enough. You want to get about double what you need in case your first attempt doesn't go according to plan. Be prepared for anything to go wrong. Blades can break or go blunt, mats can get cut through and pens can run out of ink. Take it from an old sucker; get more than you think you need.

Mat Care

Despite my constant hammering about getting extra things, I do realize that mats are expensive. It's not as if they just get handed out for free, so make sure that you take good care of your mat. You want it to be in tip top shape whenever you work with it. The most important thing to remember is not to use alcohol based products on your mat. The mat is sticky for a reason and you want it to keep its stickiness for as long as possible. The alcohol will get rid of it. I found that baby wipes are great for keeping my mat clean. Try to clean it after every use so you are ready to go with your following project and you don't have stray pieces of paper or yarn that will destroy your following project. It's kind of like leaving the dishes for the following day.

Blade Settings

On the topic of mats, let me warn you about setting your blade pressure too high. It will cut right through your mat and there is no way that you can save it. It will be ruined forever. Rather, set it to a lower setting to test it out first before you go all out. Always test first because some materials – based on humidity, temperature and quality – may be softer than others.

Easy-Tac

The time will come when your mat has lost all its stickiness and you are left with a perfectly good mat that you cannot use anymore because it's lost its stick. Fear not, fellow crafters for I have a solution for you! Simply cover the edges of your mat so you don't make the edges that aren't supposed to be sticky stick to your hands for an entire day and spray a layer of Easy-Tac on the mat. There you go! Good as new. You are welcome for this little money saving tip. It is by far one of my favorites and I wish I had known it sooner before I spent so much money on replacement mats.

Too Sticky Mat

There is a slight chance that you have a too-sticky mat. Whether it is a new mat or one you attacked with Easy-Tac, there is a way that you can get rid of this. Simply tap the mat to get rid of the stickiness a bit. The oils in your hand will make the stickiness less intense. You can also dab it on your clothes, but be sure to have a lint roller handy. Those pet hairs are not going to come off easily. Your best bet is to avoid the latter tip if you have pets.

Charge Your Phone

Let me set the scene: you are cutting your projects, waiting for the machine to finish whatever it is that it's doing and you are bored out of your mind. Your phone is dead and your charger is broken. What do you do? Use your Cricut Maker to charge your phone. The machine is so handy that there is even a slot where you can put your phone in while you are watching some of those addictive YouTube videos. This is a feature that not a lot of people know about. It's a sort of Easter egg, if you will.

Test, test, test

The thing with the Cricut machine is that you have to test, test, and test before you tackle a big project. You have to get used to your Cricut. Think of it as wiggling a faulty USB until it picks up the drive. Even after years of crafts under my belt, I still like to test projects before I give them a proper go. There are so many things that a person needs to remember when using the machine such as the pressure of the blade, speed, what mat to use, etc. It can become quite overwhelming. The best way to avoid mistakes as much as possible is to test the project out on some spare materials before you get into it and waste the fabrics paper or whatever you were going to use. This will also tell you when the mat might be a little too dirty, too sticky or not sticky enough; the blade is blunt, set too low or too high, and even how long the project will take when you are doing it properly.

Sharp Blades are Good Blades

Here is a little trick that I never knew until I read about it a few weeks ago. Aluminum foil is great for keeping your blades sharp and clean. The thing with Cricut blades is that you want them as sharp as humanly possible. That means that you have to take extra care of them or buy new blades on the regular. Now, I still like to keep a good number of blades in stock, but by using this trick, I haven't had to replace it with a new one for weeks. Here's how you do it. Ball up a piece of aluminum foil tightly. It had to be big enough for your blade to disappear in so make it as big as you can. Now, remove the blade from its housing and plunge it into the ball. I like to repeat this 50-70 times depending on how blunt the blade was before I started pushing it into the foil. The foil will restore the blade to its former glory and it's going to save you a lot of money too! I wish I learned this little trick before I got rid of so many blades over the years. This is the sort of tip people need to know at the very beginning of their Cricut journey.

Settings are Important

I cannot stress this enough; double check your settings before you start cutting. Missing a setting or accidentally putting it on the wrong one can be disastrous. Rather be a pain about it than ruin your mat or the materials you've gone out of your way to buy for certain projects.

You will thank me for this even though it seems like I am talking nonsense now. Just trust me.

Peeling Paper and Curls

You know when you are peeling a sticky note and the whole thing curls in an awkward way that pretty much makes it unusable? That happens when you peel paper from the mat the wrong way, too. The right way to do this is by peeling the mat from the paper and not the paper from the mat. I know, your mind is blown, isn't it? This will ensure that every peel is a satisfying one and you can enjoy it the same way some people enjoy ASMR. It's oddly relaxing and satisfying. Peel the right way, not the noob way and you should be A for away.

Pen Grips

So those darn sharpies just won't fit in the slot despite me telling you that you can use it. What a pity, now you have all those sharpies and you can't use them for what you bought them for. That is wrong, my crafty friend. Pen grips are great for adjusting the size of a pen or pencil to fit into the Cricut. Sure, they are out of fashion and no one uses them anymore which is why you can just collect them around your house if you've ever used them or get some from the dollar store for dirt cheap. This way you can put absolutely any pen or pencil in the designated slot without worrying about it not being stable enough.

CHAPTER 10:

Choosing the Best Materials for Your Project

Kind of Cricut Accessories You Need To Get Started Crafting with. This will have most of the things you need to make staggering projects quickly and successfully.

This contraption set incorporates:

- Turn around Tweezers to lift and check delicate materials

- Welder empowers you to remove minimal negative pieces from the structure.

- Scissors with Protective Cover

- Calculated Spatula to lift materials from the tangle without curving them

- Scrubber to sparkle materials and clean cutting mats

- Scoring Stylus to make wrinkle lines on cards

- 12" Wide Material Trimmer to exactly cut Vinyl, Iron-On, and Cardstock

- Swap Blades for Trimming

- Scoring Blade for Trimming and for adding scoring lines to different assignments

- Cricut Ultimate Tool Set

The sort of materials to be obtained.

Get a wide scope of materials so you can pick up capability with the wide collection of materials that your Cricut Maker is prepared for cutting. Coming up following are two or three the materials endorsed.

- Removable Vinyl Variety Pack 12 x 12

- Move Tape

- Regular Iron-On Rainbow Sampler

- Cardstock Rainbow Sampler 12 x 24

- Texture Sampler Pack

- Felt Sampler Pack

- 5 Pen Variety Pack

- Blade

- Scoring Wheels

Cricut Explore air Materials: What can it cut?

The Cricut Explore Air can provide materials to cut.

CANVAS

Cut Setting: Custom – Canvas 0.75mm.

You will require a common edge and StandardGrip Mat. You will, in like manner, need to add a stabilizer to the texture for a flawless and clean. I used Heat n' Bond on mine. This will require 1x go to cut through, and it cuts perfectly.

CHIPBOARD MATERIAL, 50pt

Cut Settings: Custom – Chipboard Heavy, 0.7mm

You will require a significant cut edge and StrongGrip Mat. I have in like manner used a StandardGrip Mat, and it's worked phenomenally as long as the tangle isn't smudged. It ought to do a 4x cut; in any case, things being what they are, greatly!

CHANNEL TAPE

FELT, Regular Craft Store Felt

Cut Setting: Custom – Felt w/Backing.

You will require a significant cut edge and StrongGrip Mat. Moreover, a standard sharp edge with a StandardGrip Mat and it's worked unimaginably as long as the tangle isn't messy. You will similarly need to add stabilizer to the texture for a perfect and clean.

CARDSTOCK

Cut Setting: Cardstock

You will require a common cutting edge and StandardGrip Mat. This will require 1x go to cut through, and it cuts marvelously. The nuances it can cut on paper is crazy.

Straightforwardness

Cut Setting: Custom – Transparency

You will require a standard edge and StandardGrip Mat or LightGrip Mat. Regardless of anything else, this will require 1x go to cut through, and it cuts impeccably.

COTTON

Cut Setting: Fabric.

You will require a standard edge and StandardGrip Mat. You will, in like manner, need to add a stabilizer to the texture for an organized. This will require 1x go to cut through, and it cuts faultlessly.

Fitting

Cut Setting: Custom – Create a custom setting with a cut load of 250, 4x cut.

You will require a standard edge and StandardGrip Mat, guarantee your tangle is unblemished. This will require 4x go to cut through.

Cowhide

Settings: Custom – Leather, Medium 1.8mm

You will require a standard sharp edge and StandardGrip Mat, guarantee your tangle is great. Cowhide will leave a disaster area on your bunch, use a development roller to clean. This is one of the significant things to cut. This will require 4x go to cut through.

Aluminum, Soda Can

Cut Setting: Custom – Aluminum Metal, 0.14mm.

You will require a conventional sharp edge and StandardGrip Mat. This is amazingly fun, yet be wary about sharp edges. This will require 2x go to cut through. Consider all the enjoyment of Diet Coke adventures you can make!

Balsa Wood, 1/16"

Cut Setting: Custom - make a custom setting with a cut load of 230, 5x cut.

You will require a significant cut cutting edge and StandardGrip Mat. You should run this cut twice to cut through the balsa wood.

CRICUT EASY EXPRESS MATERIALS

For quick, unsurprising, capable warmth moves that last and last! With even heat from edge to edge, direct controls, and splendid prosperity features. The Cricut EasyPress machine makes it easy to take on any glow move adventure that goes to your bearing.

HOW IT WORKS

The speed of a glowing press.

The solace of an iron.

Set time and temp

Our instinctive online Cricut Heat Guide suggests no more puzzle.

Apply heat

The consistently warmed plate infers relentless, first-class moves.

Value suffering results

Without a doubt, significantly after repeated washes, your trades will genuinely last.

CRICUT EASY PRESS 2

Your no-stress warmth press.

Proficient level execution, home-pleasing plan. Cricut EasyPress 2 passes on snappy, easy, ace quality exchanges on everything from newborn child bodysuits to big-time shirts and principles.

Advanced warmth plate structure. Stoneware secured surface and two fascinating warming segments make edge-to-edge heat for expert-level trades.

Accurate temperature control up to 400°F (205°C). Enter the recommended time and temperature settings for your HTV or Infusible Ink adventure.

Thoughtful prosperity features. Secured Safety Base guarantees your work surface; the auto-shutoff feature turns it off after 10 minutes of torpidity.

Works magnificently with Cricut splendid cutting machines. Plan and cut your image. By then, move them amazingly. It's as easy as that.

CRICUT EASY PRESS MINI

Little however solid.

It's a pocket-sized warmth press! Regardless, don't be deceived by its size. Cricut EasyPress Mini packs control in a significant number of spots – despite the most astounding articles and adventures.

The faultless shape. Just 1.92" wide and 3.25" tall, it gives an ideal tip and edge control so you can put heat exactly where you need it.

Advanced warmth plate. With an extra layer of security on its glow plate, Cricut EasyPress Mini effectively skims over bases to follow your plan.

Three easy warmth settings. It's all that you need to adhere to your artistic work for all intents and purposes any base material.

Thoughtful security features. Secured Safety Base guarantees your work surface; the auto-shutoff feature turns it off after 13 minutes of torpidity.

Various Materials You Can Cut with Cricut Machine

Considering what Materials You Can furthermore cut with Cricut? Take a gander at all these excessively superb endeavors made with such countless different materials and cut with Cricut.

Various Materials You Can Cut with Cricut

Cardstock – Utilize cardstock to make a paper sprout wreath and these too much cute cupcake wrappers for a mid-year pool party.

Vinyl – This is utilized to make this vehicle window decal.

Washi Paper – I cut out cardstock and afterward did an organizing cut in washi paper (basically a goliath sheet of washi tape). By then, I stuck the washi paper cleave down to the cardstock cut and made this truly charming pinwheel-formed standard for the pool party complex subject. It was a direct appreciation to the Cricut.

Window Cling – Yep, you can make a wide scope of fun, barely noticeable subtleties with that stuff! Right?! Take a gander at this from my buddy Jill.

Wood Veneer – Yep-would you have the option to confide in it? You can use your Cricut to evacuate small wood and do wonderful things.

Fake Leather-like. This undertaking is on my once-over point of fact!

Plug – How cool is that? You can use it to expel the attachment for things like these napkins.

Iron-On Vinyl – This is likely the thing I cut the most with mine. I revere making fun shirts with all the enjoyment things my family needs. Custom shirts in just two or three minutes can't be beaten.

Paste Foil – Fun social affair cups and structures came to be made quickly with a sheet of concrete foil and the Cricut.

There are furthermore printable magnet sheets, printable texture, printable vinyl, printable sticker paper, foil acidic corrosive inference, and workmanship foam!

CHAPTER 11:

Cricut Catridges

To start with, I'll clarify precisely what Cricut cartridges are. I'll discuss how you never again need to utilize cartridges (yippee!), yet in addition how you can in any case use them, even with the more up to date machines.

I'll tell you the best way to connect cartridges to your Cricut record, and afterward how to discover all the pictures from those cartridges in Design Space on your PC.

I quickly clarify the difference among physical and advanced cartridges, go over certain advantages and disadvantages, and answer the most regularly posed inquiries toward the end.

Cricut cartridges are sets of pictures and textual styles that are connected by a topic, similar to Halloween, the sea shore, or springtime. Each picture set can contain many pictures, textual styles, or tasks, and expenses somewhere in the range of five and thirty bucks.

With the early Cricut machines, the cartridges were plastic: physical capacity gadgets that you needed to plug into your slicing machine to utilize.

Do I Have To Utilize Cartridges For A Cricut Explore Air?

Actually no, not any longer! Acclaim Cricut, for cartridges are never again required for the different Cricut Explore models or the Cricut Maker.

The first Cricut shaper and the Cricut Expression arrangement were intended to be utilized with physical information cartridges as independent machines—ones that don't require a PC or a web association. The Expression machines can be utilized with the free PC structure programming Cricut Craft Room, yet you are as yet restricted to pictures bought through Cricut cartridges.

The entirety of the shaper models right now sold by Cricut doesn't require cartridges. In this way, if you have a Cricut Explore or the Cricut Maker, and would prefer not to need to consider a cartridge until kingdom come, you are allowed to proceed onward.

Would i be able to in any case utilize my cartridges with new Cricut machines?

A lady focuses to the cartridge opening on a Cricut Explore.

Truly! You can utilize all your old cartridges with any of the electronic Cricut machines. The heritage machines (never again sold by Cricut, for example, the Expression arrangement, can utilize the cartridges as they generally have, by truly embeddings them into the machine and utilizing the console overlay, or associating them to Cricut Craft Room to alter on a PC.

The more up to date machines, the Cricut Explore arrangement and the Cricut Maker, can totally still utilize any cartridges you have bought from Cricut. Be that as it may, first you need to interface them to your Cricut account so that you can get to them online through Cricut Design Space.

Instructions to Use Cartridges with the Cricut Explore Air 2

So as to utilize cartridges with the Cricut Explore Air 2, they should be connected to your Cricut account so you can get to them online with Design Space.

Cautioning: You can just connection a Cricut cartridge to a solitary Cricut account. Connecting a cartridge is IRREVERSIBLE: you can't fix it and you can't move it to another record. Continuously ensure you are marked into the privilege Cricut account before connecting your cartridges!

Head on over to cricut.com/plan and sign into Cricut Design Space on a Windows or Mac PC. You can't connect cartridges through the telephone or tablet applications.

Ensure your Cricut Explore is turned on and associated with your PC.

Snap the menu button in the upper left (it would appear that a cheeseburger: three level bars) and select "Connection Cartridges", mostly down the menu. In Cricut Design Space, the choice for "Connection Cartridges" is featured.

Select your Cricut gadget starting from the drop menu.

When incited, embed your cartridge into the space on the left half of the Explore shaper, over the "Open" button.

A Cricut cartridge is embedded into the opening on a Cricut Explore.

After Design Space has identified the cartridge, the green "Connection Cartridge" catch will illuminate. Snap the catch to connect your cartridge.

When the cartridge is connected to your Cricut account, Design Space will affirm "Cartridge connected." You would now be able to continue connecting the remainder of your cartridges, see your cartridges, or hit the X in the upper option to close the cartridge connecting discourse, and come back to Cricut Design Space.

How Would I Discover My Cartridges In Cricut Design Space?

It's anything but difficult to get to your connected cartridges and bought pictures in Cricut Design Space.

In an open canvas in Design Space, click the "Pictures" button on the menu bar to one side to open up the Images window.

Over the top, you'll see three interactive words: Images Categories Cartridges. Snap "Cartridges" to see a rundown of all the Cricut cartridges accessible.

If you need to see only the cartridges that you effectively possess, click the "Channel" button on the upper right of the Images window and select "My Cartridges." This will incorporate all free and bought cartridges. In Cricut Design Space, the sifting alternative for the cartridges is chosen.

Make a point to look at the Images tab also if you have bought or transferred singular pictures.

What's The Difference Among Physical And Advanced Cartridges?

Physical cartridges contain themed sets of pictures in a plastic cartridge that you truly embed into your cutting machine. With the Cricut Expression you can utilize physical cartridges straightforwardly by embeddings them into the machine and utilizing the console to choose and control the pictures. You can likewise interface these physical cartridges to your Cricut account utilizing Design Space or Craft Room. When connected, you can promptly get to computerized variants of the cartridges in the web based altering programming.

Be that as it may, you should in any case keep the physical cartridge, or if nothing else snap a couple photographs of the front and back. If you ever experience difficulty getting to your connected cartridges and need to resin them, Cricut backing may request these photographs as evidence that you possess the cartridges.

Advanced cartridges are themed sets of pictures purchased on the web, and are promptly accessible through Cricut Design Space. They have no physical segment so that nothing will be dispatched to you and nothing should be connected to your Cricut shaper. You can utilize these with all the ongoing Cricut machines when you are associated with the web and signed into Cricut Design Space.

Professionals

Cartridges are a fantasy for a learner crafter. Making your own plans without any preparation can be astounding, however some of the time it's somewhat scary taking a gander at a clear canvas and pondering where to begin. With cartridges, you can discover motivation effectively within reach, gathered by any occasion or subject you can conjure up. Cartridges are a brisk and simple approach to jump into making custom made vinyl decals and welcome cards, without spending ages fixating on the plan.

There are huge amounts of bit by bit instructional exercises you can discover to make ventures with cartridges. These are extraordinary to utilize when you are first figuring out how to utilize a Cricut. There are such a large number of different things to realize when you are beginning, instructional exercises make it simple by taking out all the mystery! Look at this overly adorable fox head produced using the 3D Animal Heads

If you want to use the Cricut like a printer in whatever ways, you can do that as well. There is an accessory slot in your machine and you can load a marker into it. From there, you can load a marker into it and have the machine draw your design for you. It is great for getting a beautifully handwritten look. This is especially helpful to people whose handwriting is not considered a strong suit for them.

Each machine has different ways of cutting things, and you will notice this depending on which machine you get. You can make different things with them as well. You can cut fun shapes for scrapbooking (this is considered a lost art or an older generation activity but it is very entertaining and a great way for preserving memories) and design T-shirts, leather bracelets, stickers for your car, or envelopes. The options are endless, and all of them are fun and can be used as business options for people as well when you are creating your own designs.

Cartridge:

The pictures in every cartridge are painstakingly chosen and well-curated. Numerous gifted craftsmen have poured huge amounts of time and exertion into the making of cartridges only for you to utilize! You can believe that the pictures and textual styles will be high-caliber, and work flawlessly with your Cricut.

There are just about 500 hundred cartridges in the Cricut Cartridge Library! Every cartridge contains different pictures and tasks that can be altered and joined with different inventive highlights, giving a phenomenal scope of plans. There are simply such a large number of shapes, examples, and text styles to browse; you can generally discover something that looks incredible for whatever venture you are making.

Cartridges really are an extraordinary worth. From only a solitary cartridge you can produce several different plans from the base pictures. If you believe that your Cricut cartridge assortment has been getting excessively expensive, invest more energy exploring different avenues regarding the cartridges you as of now have, and utilize that innovative worth.

Having a physical assortment of Cricut cartridges can be brilliant for discovering motivation for your following venture. Rather than gazing at pictures on a screen to discover something to make, you can remain off the PC and peruse through a physical library of your cartridge assortment.

Cons

Before the Cricut Explore arrangement, the principle burden of the cartridge framework was that you were constrained to what went ahead the cartridges. Since cartridges are currently totally discretionary with the more up to date Cricut machines, this is never again a detriment! You can generally transfer your own structures or utilize free SVGs you find on the web.

A charming paper craft creature head, made out of pastel cardstock.

One significant issue is that you can just connection cartridges to a solitary Cricut account. If you are gifted cartridges, or get some from e-cove or a thrift shop, they may as of now be connected to another person's record! Connecting cartridges is irreversible, and you can't switch what record they're connected to. So ensure you don't get fooled into purchasing cartridges you can't really use with your machine.

Subsequent to purchasing a lot of cartridges you may feel like you are secured in the Cricut brand, or possibly with a specific machine. This is extraordinary for Cricut, yet not all that good for offering to the making and DIY people group.

CHAPTER 12:

Frequently Asked Questions

Why can't I weed my design without it tearing?

There are two fairly common causes for this type of issue. Number one is dull blades. We have some tips on how to sharpen your blades, so just look for that! The second reason is a buildup of residues on your blades

Where do I go to buy materials?

When it comes to buying materials for your Cricut, there are nearly an unlimited number of places where you can get them. Since the Cricut is such a versatile machine with the ability to cut so many materials, you won't be able to go into any crafting or fabric stores without tripping over new materials you can use for your latest and greatest crafts.

As you continue to learn more about how Cricut works and what you can do with it, you will find which materials and brands best suit your needs. From there, you will often find what you need by shopping online to get the best prices and quantities of the materials you prefer, which will help you stretch your dollar as best as you can.

Do I need a printer to use my Cricut?

In a word, no. Using your Cricut with the materials we've laid out in this manuscript doesn't require ink from a printer, though there are some materials on the market for Cricut, which are specifically meant to be printed on before using.

If you're not using these items, then you will find that you can get the most out of your machine without that feature.

If you wish to print things, and then cut them, this is known as the Print then Cut method and there is a wealth of knowledge about this on the internet. You can make iron-on decals, tattoos, and so much more!

Where can I get images to use with my Cricut?

The beautiful thing about the Cricut Design Space and its ability to host so many different file types is that you can upload images from any source, so long as you have the legal rights to use that image. Pulling images off of Google Image Search is done amongst crafters, but if you're selling the design in any way, you will want to make sure that the images you're using are either open license, or you've purchased them for use and distribution.

Do I have to buy all my fonts through Cricut?

Cricut Design Space has an option when looking through your fonts to use fonts that are installed on your computer. This is called "System Fonts." Ant font you can buy, or download can be used through

Cricut Design Space with little to no issues. There are many resources for this on the internet as well.

However, if there is a font you're using, do make sure that you have the license to use the font for the purposes you have in mind for that font! Fonts, just like pictures, do have copyrights and can be limited in what they allow you to do with them.

Why is my blade cutting through my backing sheet?

This can be due to improper seating on the blade in the housing, so just pop the housing out, re-seat the blade inside, reload, and try again. This can also be due to an improper setting on the material dial. If you're cutting something very thin, but have the dial set to cardstock, your needle could be plunging right through the whole piece of material and its backing!

Why aren't my images showing up right on my mat?

It is possible, when you click "Make It," that the print preview of your project doesn't look anything like how you have it laid out in Design Space. If this is the case, go back to Design Space, highlight all your images, click "Group," then click "Attach." This should keep everything right where it needs to be for all your project cutting needs!

I'm just getting started; do I need to buy all of Cricut's accessories right away?

No, you won't need all the accessories right at once, and some of them you won't ever need at all, depending on what crafts you intend to do with your Cricut machine. In fact, you can use crafting items you likely already have on hand to get started, buying tools and accessories here and there as you get more use out of your machine! It is, by no means, necessary to spend a small fortune on accessories and tools just to do your first Cricut crafting project!

Which Cricut machines at compatible with design space?

The Cricut models that are currently compatible are all of the motorized cutting machines they have on the market! This means the Cricut Explore, Cricut Explore Air, Cricut Explore Air 2, and the Cricut Maker. You can use all these tools with the current version of Design Space to create countless projects for every style and occasion. Outdated machinery will need to be tested with the application to see if they're compatible, as Cricut does provide regular updates for the application that could nullify that compatibility over time.

Do I need to be linked to the internet to use design space?

Cricut Design Space is a web-based application that utilizes the cloud. Because of this, you do need an active, high-speed internet connection in order to make use of the application for your designs. However, the cloud functionality gives you access to your account, your designs, your elements, and everything within the Design Space from any device, anywhere in the world, so long as you have an internet connection and your account credentials.

Is my operating system compatible with Cricut Design Space?

Cricut Design Space is currently compatible with devices operating in the latest systems for Windows, Mac, Android, and iOS. If you have questions about your device's compatibility with the latest plugin for Cricut's Design Space, simply visit their page on system requirements and see what is listed there for you and the operating system you use.

Can I use the Design Space on more than one of my devices?

Yes, thanks to Cricut's web-based and cloud-based functionality, all of your designs, elements, fonts, purchases, and images are accessible from any device with an internet connection and your account credentials. This way, it's possible to start a design while you're out and about for the day, and then wrap them up when you're back in your crafting space.

How long can I use an image I buy in the Design Space?

Any design asset or element you purchase through the design space is yours to use as many times as you'd like while you have an active account with Cricut Design Space! Feel free to cut as many of every image you'd like!

I accidentally welded two images. How do I unweld them?

Unfortunately, there is no dedicated unweld option currently available in Design Space. If you weld an image, however, you can still click

"Undo" if you have not saved the changes to your project. It is recommended that you save your images locally at each different stage, so you have clean images to work with for every project.

How do I set design space to operate on the metric system?

On your computer (whether it's Windows or Mac), click the three stacked lines in the upper left-hand corner. From there, click "Settings." In those settings, you'll see the option to set inches or centimeters as the default measurement.

If you're using Design Space on your mobile device, you will access your settings from the bottom of your screen. You may need to roll or jab to the left to view all your options, but this setting is available on mobile as well!

What types of images can I upload through Cricut's design space iOS or Android apps?

Any images that are saved in the Photos or Gallery app on your Apple or Android device can be uploaded! If you have SVG files saved, you can upload those as well.

If you are trying to upload a .PDF or a .TIFF file, it should be noted that Cricut Design Space does not support these.

Can I upload images through the Android app?

Yes! Cricut understands how crucial mobile accessibility is to its users, so this feature has been made available on all platforms where you can access Cricut Design Space, including Android!

Can I upload photos while I'm offline?

Uploading images can only be done with an active high-speed internet connection. This is true of any platform you'll work with that is based on the web or the cloud. Once an image is uploaded, however, it can be accessed and downloaded onto other devices for offline use.

Is it possible for me to upload sewing patterns that I have made to Design Space?

Do I have to buy a Bluetooth wireless adapter purchasing a machine to explore?

If you bought the air Browse and explore atmosphere 2, you do not have to obtain a Bluetooth wireless adapter. But this is not the same for the Explore One, and so you can buy Bluetooth wireless adapter Cricut if that's what they want.

Cricut makers can know the sheet loaded without smart dialing. How?

The machine carriage moves to the right before cutting your project. This is called homing. In this case, the device will scan the page and find out what you have installed.

How to download the software Explore machines?

To do this, first, go to design.cricut.com on your laptop or computer and log on with your ID Cricut. You will be guided through the process of downloading the plug-in Space Design and install it.

It can also be used on your phone by downloading the application from Google Play Store if you are a user of Android, App Store, or if you are a user of iOS.

If I upgrade from a maker explore a Cricut, will I lose my projects and cartridges?

No, he will not. All your information is not linked to the Cricut machine. Instead, you connect to your Cricut ID cloud. While you are using the same ID, you can access all your information and projects when a new machine Cricut is obtained.

My Cricut machine must be connected to the internet?

Your Cricut machine does not work alone, but instead must be connected to the design space. Space design uses an Internet connection unless you are using the offline version on your iOS device.

How can I use the same design space for both the series and Cricut Explore Maker?

Your Design of the space is not going to change, even if you are replacing a Cricut machine to another. Also, no matter which one you are using, you always have to use the design space. But Cricut Maker has more benefits Design series exploring the area.

Conclusion

Thank you for making it to the end. Cricut machines are awesome gadgets to own because they do not only boost creativity and productivity, they can also be used to create crafts for business. With Design Space, crafters can create almost anything, and even customize their products to bear their imprints.

All over the world, people use these machines to make gift items, t-shirts, interior décor, and many other crafts, to beautify their homes, share with friends and family during holidays, and even sell, etc.

There two types of Cricut machines; the Cricut Explore and the Cricut Maker. Both machines are highly efficient in their rights, and experts in the crafting world make use of them to create a plethora of items, either as a hobby or for business.

Both machines are similar in many ways i.e. the Cricut Maker and the Explore Air 2, but the Cricut Maker is somewhat of a more advanced machine because it comes with some advanced features, as compared to the Explore Air 2.

One distinct feature about the Maker that sets it apart from the Explore Air is the fact that it can cut thicker materials. With the Maker, the possibilities are limitless and crafters can embark on projects that were never possible with Cricut machines before the release of the Make.

Another feature that puts the Cricut Maker machine ahead of the Explore Air 2 is the 'Adaptive Tool System'. With this tool, the Cricut Maker has been empowered in such a way that it will remain relevant for many years to come because it will be compatible to new blades and other accessories that Cricut will release in the foreseeable future.

Although both machines have several dissimilarities, there are also areas where they completely inseparable. Take for example the designing of projects in Cricut Design Space.

Take note that the Cricut Design Space is the software where all the magnificent designs are made before they are sent to be cut. It is one of the most important aspects in the creation of crafts in the Cricut set up. However, when it comes to Cricut Maker and the Explore Air 2, there is nothing to separate them in this regard, because both machines use the same software for project design.

As a crafter, without proper knowledge of Design Space, you're not only going to cut out poor products, you will also make little or no in-road in your quest to find success.

Understanding Design Space is important because it empowers crafters with enormous tools and materials to create generalized and custom products. It is an extremely powerful tool that just cannot be overlooked by anyone that intends to follow this path.

Thus, the understanding of Design Space is a MUST for people that intend to make a business out of Cricut machines or even utilize it as a hobby. With the software, crafters can create their designs from scratch or use already-made designs on the Cricut platform. Those that have an active subscription on Cricut Access, have access to thousands of images, projects, and fonts. They can cut out their products using these images or projects, and they can also edit them to suit their style and taste before cutting.

Cricut Design Space comes with some exciting tools and features that can make crafting easy and straightforward. These tools are not so hard to use, thus, in order to get conversant with them, you need to do some research and consistently apply the knowledge you gain from your research and reading. Expert crafters know all about the important tools in Cricut Design Space, as well as the role they play in the design of projects. Some of these tools include; the slice tool, weld tool, contour tool, attach tool and flatten tool, etc.

Cricut machines do not function separately -when you purchase them, they come with accessories and tools that are required for them to function. Minus the tools and accessories that come in the pack, there are also others can be purchased separately in order to boost the machine's functionality and output. In this book, we have discussed the basic accessories and tools that are needed for crafters to use along with their machines for optimum functionality and ease of design and production.

In terms of the Cricut Design Space software and app, some tips and tricks aid the process of project design and production. The software is easy and straightforward to learn and design on, but like every other applications and software, it still has some related issues and problems.

When problems arise, solutions are naturally proffered, and in terms of Cricut Design Space, there are several ways to address app related issues to improve user experience and functionality. This book covers several solutions to the issues related to the Design Space app and software.

The Design Space software is web based, thus, some laptop computers are perfectly suited for the purpose. These laptops are suitable for several reasons, including; speed, Space and design, etc. In summary, the best five are; Asus Vivobook F510UA, Dell Inspiron 15 5575, Lenovo Ideapad 330S, Asus Vivobook S410UN, and the Acer Aspire E 15.

Everything on earth needs maintenance, including Cricut machines. These machines are constantly cutting out materials of different textures, shapes, and quantity, etc. Thus, they need routine maintenance in order to boost their productivity levels and increase their life span.

The routine maintenance of these machines does not require a lot, and as a matter of fact, the hardware needs cleaning after cutting out materials. Thus, non-alcoholic baby wipes are highly recommended for cleaning material residue on the machines. The cutting mat is another item that needs maintenance from time to time because excessive usage without proper care reduces its stickiness.

In terms of projects, there are so many items that can be designed, and cut out from Cricut machines.

Also, these items can be sold in the crafts market for profit. Although some people use the machines for recreational purposes, there are even a higher number of people that use to for commercial purposes.

Commercial users of Cricut machines design and cut out items to sell for profit and the machines have proven to be a blast.

One of the reasons why people can sell items made from Cricut machine is because they have the option of creating custom and unique products that cannot be found anywhere else.

I hope you have learned something!

CRICUT DESIGN

SPACE:

The Ultimate Guide for Beginners and Advanced
Users. Tools, Explore Air 2 and Design Space,
Cricut Projects for all Levels, Tips & Tricks, Practical
Examples and Much More.

JADE PAPER

Table Of Contents

Introduction

Cricut Design Space is the online stage that Cricut designed to be utilized with their more up to date machines. It's not programming – you download a module on your PC (or the application on your table/telephone), and after that, you can design however much you might want.

You can utilize designs and pictures that are now transferred into Design Space or you can transfer your own!

Cricut Design Space is 100% free. You do need to make a record; however, if you would prefer not to, you don't need to spend a penny.

Cricut Design Space is an online programming program that enables you to interface with your cutting machines by means of USB or Bluetooth. It's the way you make most of the wonderful designs that will wind up on your tasks, shirts, cushions, espresso cups, and the sky is the limit from there!

As an option in contrast to making your own designs or getting them from Cricut, I regularly shop at Etsy (simply scan what you're searching for with SVG toward the end) and afterward "play with" my designs.

While they have some free pictures and textual styles incorporated with the program, there are ones that you can pay cash for. You can likewise pursue a Cricut Access Plan, which will give you access to a great many pictures and textual styles.

Be that as it may, you can introduce your own textual styles onto your PC and transfer pictures to Design Space (that you've made, found for nothing, or obtained without anyone else).

Cricut Design Space is an online program, so you don't download it onto your PC.

Nonetheless, you should download some modules, which should auto popup and brief you to download when you experience the underlying procedure.

If you are needing to download Cricut Design Space onto your iPhone or iPad, then you will simply need to go to the Apple App Store, scan for "Design Space," and it ought to be the primary alternative to spring up. Download it like you regularly would.

Any undertaking that you make in Design Space can be spared to the Cloud. You simply need to ensure you spare your venture – which catch is in the upper right hand corner.

This enables you to see your task on any gadget where you are signed in. Nonetheless, if you are dealing with an iPhone or an iPad, you have the choice to spare it just to your gadget. I would, for the most part, consistently propose sparing it to the Cloud, however!

You can utilize Design Space on Mac PCs, PC PCs, and iOS gadgets.

Your PC must run a Windows or Mac working framework, and hence, Google Chromebooks CANNOT be utilized, as they keep running on a Google OS.

Once in a while when you go to cut your design, it will stop you before you at the tangle see page and state you have to pay.

You may have incidentally included a picture that requires installment – you can return to your canvas and check each picture to check whether there is a dollar sign beside it (or check whether the text style you chose has a dollar sign. Remember that regardless of whether you have Cricut Access, you don't approach ALL the pictures and textual styles).

If you chose a venture from Design Space, it might have incorporated a picture or textual style that is paid. When you take a gander at the task guidelines, it should let you know if it is free or not.

I see this inquiry all the time in Design Space, and it very well may be so disappointing! Frequently, Design Space is down when they are making refreshes.

Some of the time, they will convey an email when they anticipate a blackout. However, I don't generally observe this.

If it's down, I would propose not reaching their client backing and simply be quiet. You can likewise attempt another program or clear your program store, just to ensure it is anything but an issue on your end.

Cutting is one of my preferred highlights in Cricut Design Space! I cherish removing text styles and pictures in different designs.

Yet, now and then it won't work. If you are observing this to be an issue, here are a couple of thoughts:

– Make sure the picture/text style you are removing of (so that is over another picture) is totally inside the other picture. If a bit of it is standing out, it won't cut.

– Make sure everything is chosen.

– Keep as a main priority that when you cut it, you will have two layers to expel from the picture – the first picture/text style that you cut, just as the cut

For what reason isn't print and cut working?

I won't jump a lot into Print and Cut, as it is a monster all alone.

Notwithstanding, the most compelling motivation why I see individuals experiencing difficulty with Print and Cut is that they didn't smooth their pictures! Before you go to print and cut, ensure you select all and press straighten.

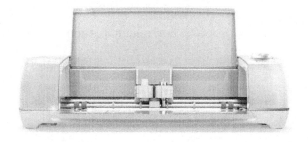

For what reason Can't I Open Cricut Design Space?

Regularly you will get a blunder or a white screen with Design Space if you don't have the most as of late refreshed module.

If you get a clear page, take a stab at invigorating the page to check whether the module update shows up. Try not to move far from this page when it's refreshing, or it will turn white.

Cartridge

Designs are produced using parts put away on cartridges. Every cartridge accompanies a console overlay and guidance booklet. The plastic console overlay demonstrates key determinations for that cartridge as it were. Anyway, as of late Provo Craft has discharged an "All-inclusive Overlay" that is perfect with all cartridges discharged after August 1, 2013. The motivation behind the all-inclusive overlay is to simplify the way toward slicing by just learning one console overlay as opposed to learning the overlay for every individual cartridge. Designs can be removed on a PC with the Cricut Design Studio programming, on a USB associated Gypsy machine, or can be legitimately inputted on the Cricut machine utilizing the console overlay. There are two kinds of cartridges shape and textual style. Every cartridge has an assortment of imaginative highlights which can take into consideration several different cuts from only one cartridge. There are as of now more than 275 cartridges that are accessible (independently from the machine), containing textual styles and shapes, with new ones included monthly. All cartridges work just with Cricut programming, must be enrolled to a solitary client for use and can't be sold or given away. A cartridge obtained for a suspended machine is probably going to wind up futile at the point the machine is ended. Cricut maintains whatever authority is needed to suspend support for certain renditions of their product whenever, which can make a few cartridges quickly out of date.

The Cricut Craft Room programming empowers clients to join pictures from different cartridges, consolidate pictures, and stretch/turn pictures; it doesn't take into account the formation of discretionary designs. It additionally empowers the client to see the pictures showed on-screen before starting the cutting procedure so that the final product can be seen in advance.

Referring to Adobe's surrender of Flash, Cricut declared it would close Cricut Craft Room on 15 July 2018. Clients of "heritage" machines were offered a markdown to refresh to models good with Cricut Design Space. Starting at 16 July 2018, Design Space is the main programming accessible to make projects. Design Space isn't perfect with cartridges once in the past bought for the Cricut Mini, which was power nightfall in October 2018.

Third-party

Provo Craft has been effectively unfriendly to the utilization of outsider programming programs that could empower Cricut proprietors to remove designs and to utilize the machine without relying upon its exclusive cartridges. In a similar audit of bite, the dust cutting machines, survey site identified being "restricted to cutting designs from a gathering of cartridges" as a noteworthy downside of the Cricut run; however, the audit noticed that it could be an inclination for some.

Two projects which could once in the past be utilized to make and after that get Cricut machines to remove subjective designs (utilizing, for instance, self-assertive TrueType text styles or SVG group illustrations) were Make-the-Cut (MTC) and Craft Edge's Sure Cuts A Lot (SCAL). In April 2010 Provo Craft opened lawful activity against the distributers of Make-the-Cut, and in January 2011 it sued Craft Edge to stop the conveyance of the SCAL program. In the two cases, the distributers settled with Provo Craft and expelled support for Cricut from their items. The projects keep on being usable with other home cutters.

As indicated by the content of its lawful grumbling against Craft Edge, "Provo Craft utilizes different strategies to encode and cloud the USB correspondences between Cricut Design Studio [a design program provided with the hardware] and the Cricut e-shaper, so as to secure Provo Craft's restrictive programming and firmware, and to avoid endeavors to capture the cutting commands". Provo Craft battled that so as to comprehend and imitate this darkened convention, Craft Edge had dismantled the Design Studio program, in opposition to the provisions of its End User License Agreement, along these lines (the organization affirmed) breaking copyright law. Provo Craft additionally affirmed that Craft Edge was damaging its trademark in "Cricut" by saying that its product could work with Cricut machines. Provo Craft declared this was likely "to cause perplexity, misstep or double dealing with regards to the source or starting point of Defendant's merchandise or benefits, and [was] prone to erroneously recommend a sponsorship, association, permit, or relationship of Defendant's products and ventures with Provo Craft."

CHAPTER 1:

Machine Setup

Setting up your machine could look somehow complicated or tedious. However, this unit is majorly written to guide you through it; the unboxing process and the setting up. So, relax and bring that Cricut machine out wherever you've stashed it. It takes approximately 1 hour to finish setting up a Cricut machine. With this guide, you should be done in less than an hour. Let's get right on it, shall we?

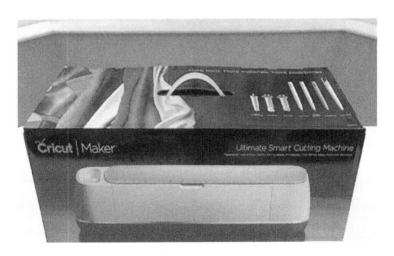

STEP 1: OPENING THE BOX

To make sure that we are together all the way through, we will go through even the most trivial step; opening the box.

You should be having a number of boxes right now in front of you if you went for the whole Cricut bundle. And there should be a big box among those boxes which contains the Cricut machine itself. If you open that big box, the first thing you should find is a Welcome packet; most of the tools will be in that packet. You should find a welcome manuscript, rotary blade and cover, a USB cable, a fine-point pen, a packet that contains your first die-cutting project. The USB cable is sometimes the last thing you'll see in this packet, it's hidden under every other stuff. Underneath this welcome packet is your Cricut machine.

To find the power cable, you first need to bring out the machine out from its box. You will then discover the power cable underneath the box with two cutting mats of standard sizes. That looked easy, right? Let's proceed to the following step.

STEP 2: UNWRAPPING YOUR CRICUT MACHINE AND SUPPLIES

We are getting to the exciting part. Let's unwrap your machine and find out what's inside.

When trying to unwrap your machine, you'll find it covered in a protective wrapper that looks filmy and also with a cellophane layer. Try to carefully unwrap the top foam layer so you can see the machine clearly. After that, go on to remove the remaining part of the Styrofoam that protects the inner machine housing.

When you unbox the whole casing, you should expect to find the following tools;

Cricut Machine

USB and Power Cables

Rotatory blade with housing.

Fine point blade with housing

Fine point pen.

Light-Grip and Fabric-Grip Mats (12 x 12)

STEP 3: SETTING UP YOUR MACHINE

Finally, we can move on to getting your machine up and running. Most of what you'll be doing will be technically inclined. You basically need electricity, a mobile phone or computer with internet access. Once you have access to all these, plug your power cord into an electronic outlet and then switch on your machine.

I'll assume your Cricut machine has Bluetooth function. If it does not have this function, either make use of the USB cable to connect your computer and the Cricut machine or purchase a Bluetooth adapter as soon as you can.

Once they are all connected, open your computer browser to continue the setup. Visit the Cricut Sign-in Page and click on the "Sign in" icon. You will have to either sign in with your account details or create a new account for yourself if you don't already have one. This is necessary so as to be able to access the Cricut Design Space.

Sign In

Cricut ID*

your email address

Password*

Remember Me   Forgot Password?

Sign In

Create a Cricut ID

. Faster Checkout

. Save multiple shipping addresses

. View and track orders and more

Create Cricut ID

If you do not have an active account yet, don't bother to fill any information on the sign-in fields. Click on the "Create Cricut ID" in the green box and then fill out every field with the required information and click on "Submit."

Create a Cricut ID

Your Cricut ID is your golden ticket to all things Cricut.

First Name

Last Name

Country
Please select

☐ I accept the Cricut Terms of Use
☑ Send me free inspiration & exclusive offers

Email / Cricut ID

Retype Email / Cricut ID

Password

Already have a Cricut ID?
Sign In

Now, it's time to link your machine to your account. It takes some people a lot of time to finish this part successfully. To make it easier, follow the procedures below.

After signing in, go to the upper left corner of the page and click on the drop-down menu icon (with three lines) beside "Home."

When the drop-down menu appears, select the "New Machine Setup."

On the following screen that pops up, click on your Cricut machine model.

Another webpage will appear with instructions on how to connect your machine. Follow the instruction accordingly.

When you follow the instructions, it automatically detects your machine and prompts you to download and install the software.

The site is user-friendly, so you'll be directed on how to go about the installation. And if you already have an account, you may still need to download it again. Cricut updates their design space often, there could be some new tools in the latest version that you don't have access to. It only takes about five minutes to get the installation done.

And there we go; we have concluded the setup procedure on your PC. That wasn't too hard, was it?

You might find the software a little bit complex for you when you first start to explore it. But with constant usage, you'll master it.

STEP 4: CLAIMING YOUR BONUS

When you have successfully created an active account on Cricut, you can claim access to Cricut for a whole month for free! It's a welcome bonus from Cricut. You'll have access to different projects, fonts, as well as Cut files. You can exploit this opportunity by making use of the accessible library to work on several fun projects.

STEP 5: COMMENCING YOUR FIRST PROJECT

You may want to start practicing with some old projects done by other people or study how they are done before you initiate your personal project. Every Cricut machine comes with a trivial project. You'll find it in the welcome pack. You can use this to get familiar with the tools the machine came with.

It may be challenging to make use of the Cricut Design Space without fully knowing its environment. So, stick with small projects till you get better, or ask someone who has more knowledge and experience with Cricut tools to guide you through.

CHAPTER 2:

Cricut Explore Air and Design Space

The Cricut Explore Air is the subsequent stage up from the Explore One. It also comes the standard Fine-Point Blade which enables you to cut several materials, and it's good with the Deep Point Blade and the Bonded Fabric Blade (sold independently) to enable you to cut considerably more materials.

One major redesign over the Explore One is that the Cricut Explore Air has a double apparatus holder; it is intended to hold a cutting edge in one clamp and a pen, scoring stylus, or another embellishment in the other clip. This implies if you have a project that has both writing and cutting, you can stack a sharp edge and a pen into the machine and it will cut and write across the board go without stopping for you to change between instruments. Far better, the second clasp is perfect with tools like the Scoring Stylus, Cricut Pens, and so on so there's no reason to buy an extra connector.

The Cricut Explore Air also offers worked in Bluetooth abilities. For the initial step, you should associate utilizing the USB link gave, yet after the underlying matching, you'll have the option to interface with your machine and cut remotely.

Features

- With double cartridge to cut, compose or score simultaneously

- With inserted Bluetooth, so you can work remotely

- Will cut in excess of 60 distinct materials

- With incorporated stockpiling segments

- Good with .svg, .jpg, .png, .bmp, .gif, .dxf documents

- Will take a shot at all Cricut cartridges

Pros

- Cut and compose, cut and score simultaneously

- You can work remotely

- Store pens, blades and different frill away compartments

- You can utilize your very own pictures or utilize any picture from the tremendous library

- Works with Cricut cartridges

Cons

- You have to buy extra apparatuses and accessories

- You have to buy fonts and designs

Cricut Explore One

The Cricut Explore One is Circuits' entrance level spending machine; it's ideal for any individual who needs to begin with a digital die cutting machine yet wouldn't like to spend a huge amount of cash. It accompanies the standard Fine-Point Blade which enables you to cut several materials, and it's perfect with the Deep Point Blade and the Bonded Fabric Blade (sold independently) to enable you to cut considerably more materials.

As its name suggests, the Explore One has a single apparatus holder, so if you need to cut and write in a similar project you should change out the sharp edge for a pen mid-route through the cut. It's extremely simple to change out the accessory or blade, and the Design Space programming will stop the slice and walk you through it when now is the right time, yet if you do a lot of tasks that join cutting, composing, or scoring, it can get tiresome sooner.

Moreover, really, the single tools holder is good with the standard estimated edges (Fine-Point, Deep Point, and Bonded Fabric), however to utilize different instruments and extras, you'll have to buy a different connector to fit in the single device holder.

The Explore One doesn't have worked in Bluetooth capacities, so you need to connect the machine to your gadget with the USB link gave. Or then again you can buy a Bluetooth connector independently to enable the machine to cut remotely.

Features

·	Utilize the Cricut Design Space for PC, Mac, iPad or iPhone

·	Transfer your own plans for nothing or pick one from the Cricut Image Library

·	Use text styles introduced from your PC

·	Work on various materials from flimsy paper to thick vinyl

·	With helpful device and extras holder

·	Works remotely by including a remote Bluetooth connector

·	No compelling reason to set with the Smart Set dial or make your very own custom settings

·	Make extends in minutes

Pros

·	Works remotely with Bluetooth connector

·	Transfer your very own pictures and structures for nothing

·	With 50,000+ pictures and text styles from Cricut Image Library

·	No settings required with the Smart Set dial

·	Prints and cuts quick

·	Structure with your very own gadget or PC utilizing Design Space

Cons

- It expenses to utilize pictures beginning at $0.99

- Bluetooth connector sold independently

CHAPTER 3:

Projects Design for Beginners the Basic

When starting a new project, you'll want to know what that project will be and what materials you will be using before doing anything else.

For example, if you want to cut vinyl letters to place on wood, you'll need to know all of your dimensions so your letters fit evenly and centered on the wood. You'll need wood that vinyl can adhere to without the risk of peeling. And you'll want to make certain that your wood is sanded and finished to your desire because you don't want any imperfections. You may find even with store-bought wood pieces advertised as ready-to-use, there are tiny imperfections.

You want to make sure when working with fabric that you know what inks or vinyls will adhere to the surface. You don't want any peeling or cracking to happen to your beautiful design.

When working with any kind of fabric, including canvas bags, you'll want to prewash for sizing because shrinkage after your design has been set can cause the design to become distorted.

If you aren't sure exactly what you want to do, have something in mind so that you aren't wasting a lot of materials by trial and error.

The cost of crafting materials can add up, so you'll want to eliminate as much potential waste as possible.

If you're new to Cricut Design Space, start with something simple. That's the worst thing you can do when you learn any new craft. There are many used Cricut machines for sale, and while some users sell because they upgraded, others are users who gave up. You made the investment and you'll want to get a return on that investment.

Project for Beginners

Leafy Garland

Garlands are an easy way to spruce up any space, and there is an infinite variety of them. Create a unique leafy one to give your home a more naturalistic feel! Feel free to change the colors of the leaves to suit you, whether you stick with green or go a little more unnatural. Tweaking the size of the bundles you make and how close you put them together will change the look of the garland. You can use different types of leaves as well. Experiment a little bit to see what you like best. Bending the leaves down the center and curling the edges a little will give you a more realistic look, or you can leave them flat for a handmade look. You can use the Cricut Explore One, Cricut Explore Air 2, or Cricut Maker for this project.

Supplies Needed

Cardstock – 2 or more colors of green, or white to paint yourself

Glue gun

Lightstick cutting mat

Weeding tool or pick

Floral wire

Floral tape

Instructions

Open Cricut Design Space and create a new project.

Select the "Image" button in the lower left-hand corner and search for "leaf collage."

Select the image of leaves and click "Insert."

Place your cardstock on the cutting mat.

Send the design to your Cricut.

Remove the outer edge of the paper, leaving the leaves on the mat.

Use a pick or scoring tool to score down the center of each leaf lightly.

Use your weeding tool or carefully pick to remove the leaves from the mat.

Gently bend each leaf at the scoreline.

Glue the leaves into bunches of two or three.

Cut a length of floral wire to your desired garland size, and wrap the ends with floral tape.

Attach the leaf bunches to the wire using the floral tape.

Continue attaching leaves until you have a garland of the size you want. Bundle lots of leaves for a really full look, or spread them out to be sparser.

Create hooks at the ends of the garland with floral wire.

Hang your beautiful leaf garland wherever you'd like!

Easy Envelope Addressing

Christmas cards are wonderful to send out, but they can take forever to address. Address labels just don't look as personal, though. Use the Cricut pen tool in your machine to "hand letter" your envelopes! You can use this for your batch of holiday cards or even for other cards or letters. This takes advantage of the writing function of your Cricut machine. For the most realistic written look, make sure you select a font in the writing style. It will still write other fonts, but it will only create an outline of them, which is a different look you could go for! Cricut offers a variety of Pen Tools, and there are some other pens that will fit as well. For addressing envelopes, stick to black or another color that is easy to read so that the mail makes it to its destination. You can use the Cricut Explore One, Cricut Explore Air 2, or Cricut Maker for this project.

Supplies Needed

Envelopes to address

Cricut Pen Tool

Lightstick cutting mat

Instructions

Open Cricut Design Space and create a new project.

Create a box the appropriate size for your envelopes.

Select the "Text" button in the lower left-hand corner.

Choose one handwriting font for a uniform look or different fonts for each line to mix it up.

Type your return address in the upper left-hand corner of the design.

Type the "to" address in the center of the design.

Insert your Cricut pen into the auxiliary holder of your Cricut, making sure it is secure.

Place your cardstock on the cutting mat.

Send the design to your Cricut.

Remove your envelope and repeat as needed.

Send out your "hand-lettered" envelopes!

Easy Lacey Dress

Lace dresses are adorable, but they can be hard to get ahold of and difficult to make. Fake it without anyone knowing better using your Cricut! The iron-on vinyl will look just like lace, and it will stand up to your child's activities much better than the real thing. Don't limit yourself to children's clothes; add some vinyl lace to your own as well! White vinyl will look like traditional lace the most, you can do this in any color that coordinates with the dress that you have. Use a Cricut EasyPress or iron to attach the vinyl to the fabric. You can use the

Cricut Explore One, Cricut Explore Air 2, or Cricut Maker for this project.

Supplies Needed

Dress of your choice

White heat transfer vinyl

Cricut EasyPress or iron

Cutting mat

Weeding tool or pick

Instructions

Open Cricut Design Space and create a new project.

Select the "Image" button in the lower left-hand corner and search "vintage lace border."

Choose your favorite lace border and click "Insert."

Place your vinyl on the cutting mat.

Send the design to your Cricut.

Use a weeding tool or pick to remove the excess vinyl from the design.

Place the design along the hem of the dress with the plastic side up. Add lace wherever you like, such as along the collar or sleeves.

Carefully iron on the design.

After cooling, peel away the plastic by rolling it.

Dress your child up in her adorable lacey dress!

Paw Print Socks

Socks are the ultimate cozy item. No warm pajamas are complete without a pair! Add a cute, hidden accent to the bottom of your or your child's socks with little paw prints. Show off your love for your pet or animals, in general, every time you cuddle up! You can do this with almost any small design or even use text to add a quote to the bottom of your feet. You can use any type of socks you find comfortable. For the easiest read, make sure the sock color and vinyl color contrast. Or, make them in the same color for a hidden design! The shine of the vinyl will stand out from the cloth in certain lights. Since this uses heat transfer vinyl, you'll need your Cricut EasyPress or iron. You can use the Cricut Explore One, Cricut Air 2, or Cricut Maker for this project.

Supplies Needed

Socks

Heat transfer vinyl

Cutting mat

Scrap cardboard

Weeding tool or pick

Cricut EasyPress or iron

Instructions

Open Cricut Design Space and create a new project.

Select the "Image" button in the lower left-hand corner and search "paw prints."

Select the paw prints of your choice and click "Insert."

Place the iron-on material on the mat.

Send the design to the Cricut.

Use the weeding tool or pick to remove excess material.

Remove the material from the mat.

Fit the scrap cardboard inside of the socks.

Place the iron-on material on the bottom of the socks.

Use the EasyPress to adhere it to the iron-on material.

After cooling, remove the cardboard from the socks.

Wear your cute paw print socks!

CHAPTER 4:

Tools in Cricut Design Space

A cricut research machine may cut pretty much anything so long as it's 2.0mm thick or thinner. And in case you've got a cricut maker, that device has one0x the cutting force and also may cut stuff up to 2.4mm thick!

Cardstock and paper

The cricut is good at cutting paper and cardstock, but it does not only cut scrapbook paper!

Vinyl

One other fantastic substance the cricut machine may cut is vinyl. Vinyl is awesome for creating signs, stickers, stencils, images, etc...

Iron on vinyl, also called heat transport vinyl, is just one of my favorite substances to cut with my cricut! You are able to use iron vinyl to decorate t-shirts, tote bags, or some other cloth item.

- flocked iron about

- foil iron on

- glitter iron on

- glossy iron on

- holographic sparkle iron about

- matte iron on

- metallic iron on

- neon iron on

- printable iron on

- Fabrics and textiles

The cricut does a fantastic job at cutting edge fabrics, but you certainly need to add a stabilizer such as wonder beneath or heat'n bond prior to cutting. These cloths and fabrics can be trimmed using a cricut research machine, however you will find even more which it is possible to cut together with the rotary blade onto a cricut maker machine.

- burlap

- canvas

- cotton fabric

- denim

- duck fabric

- faux leather

- faux suede

- felt

- flannel

- leather

- linen

- metallic leather

- oil fabric

- polyester

- printable fabric

- silk

- wool felt

Additional materials

Besides cloth, paper, and vinyl, there are tons of additional specialization stuff a cricut can cut also.

Cricut maker

In case you've got the maker, then you are able to cut more stuff! The cricut maker has one0x the cutting edge force of the research machines; also it's a rotary blade along with a knife blade which let it cut more stuff. The cricut maker may cut stuff up to 2.4mm thick, and over one25+ kinds of cloth, such as:

- chiffon

- cashmere

- fleece

- jersey

- jute

- knits

- moleskin

- muslin

- seersucker

- terry cloth

- tulle

- tweed

- velvet

- Iron on vinyl

Iron on vinyl is mainly utilized on matters which are cloth based in certain way like t-shirts, bags, fabric scraps etc...

Iron on vinyl (a.k.a heat transport vinyl or htv) is an absolute favorite for many cricut users and functions nicely with a fine-point blade, however, what exactly are a few of the best iron on vinyls to utilize?

1. Cricut heat transfer vinyl -- cricut's vinyls are excellent as they're created for cricut and from cricut. They also offer you an enormous selection of shades and textures like glitter.

2. My vinyl immediate -- vinyl direct includes a good deal more than only htv, so I'll direct you back to it over once. They have loads of patterns, colors and textures to store!

3. Firefly heat transport vinyl -- firefly is a widely known and reliable manufacturer. Does it have good appraisals but they also have a great choice! And if you're seeking good fuzzy flocked vinyl or gloss vinyl they are you covered!

4. Fame heat transport vinyl -- this new is great once you're searching for a large choice of colors. Another advantage of this new brand is the fact that it's cheaper than some choices if you're on a budget!

Mat to utilize: normally the typical grip mat will operate with vinyls.

Adhesive vinyl -- use vinyl putting

Glue vinyl is a snug favorite into the htv. There are an infinite number of applications for glue vinyl like wall stickers, mugs, decorations, boxes, wall art etc... Below are a few of the greatest brands beneath for av!

There are basically two types of glue vinyl -- durable exterior and detachable indoor -- with numerous types within each class. Vinyl will continually be described among those types and also you ought to use accordingly to this job for the best results.

By way of example, removable adhesive vinyl could work good as a detachable wall decal while durable vinyl will function better to get a timber signal you intend to hang in your door.

For glue vinyl you will generally utilize the plastic placing on your own cricut.

1. Oracal vinyl -- this vinyl is my own top option once i am considering starting a glue plastic undertaking. Oracle is thought of as the market leader when it comes to craft vinyl. This vinyl is designed to last decades. You could even locate traces of the on vinyl direct here in either matte or polished!

2. Cricut adhesive vinyl -- cricut remains a fantastic go to source for av. As an entire cricut does are far pricey but there are times that i discover a much better color in a color I'm looking for using cricut's vinyl.

3. Expressions vinyl -- expressions vinyl is another popular and user friendly. They've a fantastic color choice of glitter too!

4. Joyful crafters -- frankly this is only a joyful place site -- you may discover vinyl of all kinds and several other craft related materials!

Mat to utilize: standard grip function as well for glue vinyl.

Cardstock

Paper and cardstock are close and dear to me since i like to create paper flowers. Actually, you can access my entire library of snacks when you register!

1. Recollections cardstock -- recollections is a new by Michael's craft store, but they could also be found on the internet! I use this particular brand the very best for my newspaper crafts.

2. Savage universal newspaper rolls -- I recently found just how wonderful savage paper functions for paper crafting. Though it sounds somewhat expensive upfront, it lasts a lot more!

3. Paper and much more -- paper and more is a trustworthy source I've used and I really like the unique colors that they have.

4. Cards and pockets -- this website was with me for many years and therefore, the color choices are unparalleled to many.

Mat to utilize for cardstock paper: standard grip

Added fine-point blade materials

Let us also cover additional substances that work together with the fine-point blade and also the standard grip mat:

Lean chipboard -- great for wreathes or big letter or number workouts. Establish dial to habit and choose chipboard.

Lean poster board -- utilize for jobs with wallpapers or large cut outs. Dial ought to be put to poster board.

Stencil sheets -- produce your own customer stencils along with your cricut! I have employed the cardstock setting for stencil substance but should you purchase a different brand which is thicker than 6 mil you will to go up on the strain.

Sticker newspaper or tattoo newspaper -- should you're using the cut and print attribute, look at doing it on tattoo or decal paper for an enjoyable undertaking. I love to reduce my planner decals! Utilize the cardstock setting for all these as well with the fine-point blade.

Vellum -- vellum is simply another kind of newspaper that's usually delicate and translucent. It works excellent for any variety of paper crafts. For vellum, be certain that you place the dial to vinyl or paper.

Cellophane -- each currently and I locate a job I'm generating needs a flexible and transparent like substance -- cellophane works good for this along with also your cricut can cut it! Cellophane will have to get cut in the lightest setting, typically the one dot before it.

Deep-cut blade -- which can I trim?

For all the substances below you will want to place your machine or dial to custom and research the title of the content to place the appropriate cut strain.

Chipboard -- should you will need a thicker chipboard then exactly what the fine-point blade can manage, and then place your deep cut blade to get the job done!

Rubber -- want to create your own stamps? You can with this fantastic rubber along with also the deep-cut blade.

Wood veneer antiques -- you could have the ability to use a fine-point blade together with the timber veneer if it's thin , but likely will need the profound blade ordinarily.

Magnets -- making your own magnets could be really enjoyable. A fantastic teacher appreciation present in reality.

Leather -- leather is the rage at this time, particularly those snazzy leather earrings!

Craft foam -- foam is particularly wonderful for children crafts. Pre-cut a lot of fun shapes and also have your children enjoy some catchy fun time!

Mat board -- mat board is essential cardboard however nicer. So any project that you would like to use cardboard can work together with the profound cut blade!

Felt sheets -- love sensed blossoms or crafts? Then let your cricut perform the job for you! You might also conduct stiffened sheets!

Glitter cardstock -- I really like my glitter cardstock to get a sorts of endeavors. I've cut it using the fine-point blade although the profound works especially with all the chunky glitter paper. Craft shops frequently have some or utilize the link I supplied!

Preferences: for the stuff in this segment you may probably choose habit for a lot of them and specify in design space which you are using on the trim display. Layout space includes a setting for these choices.

Fabric blade -- what do I cut?

The cloth blade is pretty unique to cloth and you'll generally keep the cloth setting set up on the dial. Listed below are a couple of my favorite fabric areas to store. You might also cut cloth using the two former blades i advise giving the cloth intended blade a go! Spoonflower -- if you want a good deal of cloth to select from or to custom design your own cloth in a few short clicks afterward spoonflower is your thing to do! Joann fabrics -- most of you have likely heard of Joann's fabrics. They've been around quite a while and a number of you might have a shop nearby. If you do not, you can store here online!

Fabric immediate -- if you would like a significant website filled with cloth and at wholesale rates, then make sure you check out cloth direct. I've bought velvet from them for a few autumn pumpkin crafts and adored it!

Mat to utilize: fabric grip mat or regular grip.

Knife blade (cricut maker just) -- what do I cut?

Together with the knife blade (cricut maker just) you can cut a great deal of similar cricut substances as with the profound sword but the difference is that it may cut 2-3x thicker stuff then the research can deal with!

Thick leather -- the knife blade was commended for how well and wash it cuts thicker leather substances. Therefore, in the occurrence that you would like to earn those stylish leather earrings or perhaps a clutch handbag then this really is exciting! Incidentally check out this golden and silver leather!

Thick chipboard -- should you desire a heftier chipboard material that the knife blade may take can of this.

CHAPTER 5:

Intermediate and Advanced Level Projects

When you begin to venture into the types of projects needing more expertise, you will find that you need to branch out to websites providing their own design and cutting files that you can use to create more and more imaginative stuff. For this reason, I would suggest searching for various online tools for projects you can do to expand your horizons when it comes to more complex projects! There's a list of 100 crafts you can do with your Cricut device to really make your crafts special to you to give you some ideas to get you started on where to look!

3D Wood Puzzles

You may have seen these in the museum gift shops or in the brainy kids ' toy store unit. Both are incredibly fun and, when put together, they make for a fantastic final product.

3D Foam Puzzles

For 3D puzzles, foam is just as strong so you can take them apart, bring them back together, knock them down, and more, and they bounce back.

These make such a wonderful gift to young people.

3D Wall Art

Art that pops off the wall and gives a message to all the guests about who you are is something that people pay a lot of money to have. Put on your wall a little bit of your artistic self, and show off your imagination!

Aprons

If you're a kitchen enthusiast, your apron is a perfect way to add a customized touch to your experience. You can completely own the kitchen with a character that you love, a funny saying, or just a monogram.

Banners

Any occasion with a banner is more official! Using Cricut, you can use your resources to create a special banner that will remember the opportunity at hand beautifully.

Beanies

A knit cap is a perfect way to stay warm for any outdoor activity that's going to happen during the winter months. Getting one on the side emblazoned with your own logo is sure not only to elevate the hat style but also to make many wonders where they can get one like it!

Beer Steins

Sometimes, the dollar store may have blank glass beer mugs that literally call out to craftsmen to decorate them. Create a memorable gift in your life for the beer lover!

Bookmarks

Bookmarks are such an easy craft, but they are needed almost always! If your circle is like mine, everyone around you is still in the middle of reading a manuscript. Replace the supermarket receipt with something fun and personal in the center of their novel!

Bumper Stickers

There will still be something of a theme to greet the drivers behind you in traffic. Create some fun comments to put on a bumper for you and your mates.

Business Cards

It can be so costly to get business cards made from premium stock and in unusual shapes. Printing the designs using a regular printer on cardstock and cutting out complex designs are sure to catch the attention of potential clients.

Cake Toppers

Did you come up with a fun birthday party? Using plastic or metal to make a gorgeously decorated cake topper that will blow your guests away.

167

Calendars

No matter how the times advance, you must always know which day it is! See if you can make exclusive calendars for your desk or office!

Candles

Yeah, you can't make your Cricut candles yourself. But you could get a candle in a blank glass holder and put something Beautiful on the outside of it for any occasion. Let me tell you these make perfect gifts.

Canvas Tote Bags

Tote bags are among the Planet's most popular accessories. Keep all your things together, and add some Cricut style to it! Heck, you could get some canvas if you felt like it, and make your own tote bag!

Car Decals

Did you have a business? Tell that to the universe as you fly through your week!

Centerpieces

Any large-scale event could take advantage of themed centerpieces to entertain and wow your guests!

Clothing

Put your artistic flourish with Cricut and the various materials they have to give on something that you own. Whether it is an iron-on decal or an embellishment of a dress, there is no lack of ways to please.

Coasters

Like so many other stuffs on this list, coasters will make such a perfect housewarming or holiday gift. All should use a specific set of coasters to maintain safe and dry surfaces!

Coffee Mugs

Coffee mugs are probably the only dish in my house. I'll ever want more when I see them. They're great for so many things, and you're the ideal addition to every office or kitchen, having ones that are original.

Coloring Pages

You can download line art using the pen on your Cricut to make coloring pages of any type or theme for yourself or your loved ones! If you have kids coming to visit your family, that makes for a great group activity!

Commemorative Plates

Do you know that materials from Cricut that can stick to ceramics could make a perfect decoration for commemorative plate decoration? What times do you remember?

Craft Foam Shape Sets. Much as with the puzzle sets, you can cut out craft foam just about any shape you like. Doing so with an adhesive backrest on the foam sheets will allow you to make your own little sewing sets of whatever themes you want! This requires letters too!

Decorative Plaques

Just as you saw in the segment on Cricut Projects for Beginners, decorative plaques are a breeze, and you will become more detailed and artistic as you acquire more experience with the Cricut method.

DIY Craft Kits

Creating the Cricut parts for crafting kits is a breeze. Let your imagination run wild on what bits you should put together to create your own design ideas for others! Let your judgments run rough on this one as they make perfect party favors, children's or crafts gifts, and so much more!

DIY Decals

You may put the decals you make on a carrier or backing sheet to be given out. If you don't want to put your decal right on it, simply top up with a transfer tape piece and give it away!

Doilies

Cricut's intricate designs allow you to create doilies with so many different fabrics, colors, sizes, shapes, themes, and more!

174

Envelopes

by heartfeltcreations.us design team member Archana Joshi

Were you aware that envelopes are made of one continuous piece of paper that is simply cut, folded, and glued in a particular way? This means you can take any piece of paper you want, print whatever you want, and make an envelope from it! Go crazy. Go crazy.

Flowerpots

A flower pot can be a kind of worldly object. However, they can turn into something that perfectly suits your decor with some craft paint and a stencil that you made with your Cricut, or with a decal!

Framed Affirmations

This is a difficult life! Affirmations you can put in your own font or style will make all the difference from a personal space in the vibe you receive. Jazz up your own and put it all over your house!

Gift Card Envelopes

It can really be achieved with scrapbooking paper, construction paper, foil paper, or whatever. You can turn this tiny little gift into something that everyone would love to have, very personal.

Gift Tags

As you've seen in the segment on Cricut Projects for Beginners, these tags can take on any simple gift and give it such imaginative pop. Going the little bit extra for making someone look like a gift and feeling special really makes a difference.

Greeting Cards

Many of the supermarket's most beautiful greeting cards will cost you about $9 a card these days! You can make cards that are just stunning, multi-layered, with the materials to hand in at your carving station and make them bear your personal message. It makes the whole gift so personalized and meaningful.

Hats

There are designs for making your own hats, and you can also make decals that will make an existing hat pop!

Holiday Décor

I can't even be frank about how crazy I have been in this group. There are so many decorations you can make for every event that you really can't even imagine doing them all for a holiday!

Hoodies

Perhaps nothing is more convenient than a sexy, thick hoodie. Put your own personal touch on a hoodie, or bring your favorite characters or phrases around the label.

Jewelry

Oh right. With the products available through Cricut, you can totally make your own jewelry. Leather, cloth, metal. There is everything.

Keepsake Boxes

Any art is full if it cannot be connected back to hold sake boxes in some way, right? They are all over the crafting world, and you can make boxes for keepsake or simply decorate them to the nines.

Key Fobs

Make your keys stand out by making an adorable or stylish fey fob!

Keychains

Got a favorite character or emoji? Make a keychain!

Labeled Kitchenware.

From canisters to kitchen crocks, there's nothing you can't decal!

Labels

If organizing is your weapon, using Cricut will help you make beautiful labels for every room in the house!

Lanyards

Keep your keys or ID cards displayed with style and comfort.

Leather Accents

Leather accessories can also elevate your designs from looking fantastic to look fully professional, from scrapbooking to home décor.

Leather Accessories

Wrist bands, belts, lanyards, cash clips, etc. Your Cricut will turn leather sheets into your prettiest, most stylish accessories.

Luggage Tags

Just rest assured which bag you are on the carousel. Design as much as you can a luggage tag that stands out from the crowd and claim your bag in no time!

Magnetic Poetry Sets

You can produce a series of magnetic poems and limericks on your doors, fridges, or metal tables by printing words onto a collection of printable magnets!

Magnetic Puzzles

Puzzles are an ever-enjoyable timeless gift. Print a loved one's image onto a printable magnet, make a jigsaw puzzle, and build a beautiful package for your front refrigerator or a friend!

Magnetic Storytelling Sets

You can build a series of magnetic stories and jokes on your doors, fridges, or metal tables by printing words onto a collection of printable magnets!

Magnets

Think outside the box and make your own magnetic designs, then cut them into unique shapes to place your own style on your fridge or door.

Makeup Bags

Customizing a basic zippered bag will make the item all the difference in style! Call them. Yours! You might even use your Cricut to make your own zippered bag, and then decorate it!

Mandala Decals

Mandalas are amazing, and Cricut is the ideal device to help you make decals to put on about anything.

Mason Jars

Mason jars are perfect for anything from drinking to decoration, so with this one, the sky is the limit! See what exclusive things you might put on yours.

Monogram Decals

Render it with monograms on all of your accessories very uniquely.

Name Plates

Crafter in Hand. Crafter Extraordinaire, Caren Smith. The Big Cheese. If you want people on your desk or workplace to see, it can happen!

CHAPTER 6:

Cut Vinyl with a Cricut Machine

Vinyl is self-evident, and kid did I have NO clue that there was such a significant number of. I have kept my utilization of vinyl entirely basic as of not long ago, just utilizing regular classic vinyl. However, I can't hold back to give a shot such a significant number of these vinyl choices underneath.

You can likewise utilize the Deep Cut Blade for thick cardstock and cardboards.

- Adhesive Vinyl

- Chalkboard Vinyl

- Dry Erase Vinyl

- Glitter Vinyl

- Metallic Vinyl

- Outdoor Vinyl

- Printable Vinyl

- Stencil Vinyl

- Glossy Vinyl

- Holographic Vinyl

- Matte Vinyl

The Best Materials for Cricut Explore and Maker

Iron-on vinyl

Iron-on vinyl is transcendently utilized on things that are fabric situated somehow or another, for example, shirts, totes, cloth napkins and so on.

For iron-on vinyl make certain to utilize the iron-on setting on your Cricut.

Iron-on vinyl (a.m. heat transfer vinyl or HTV) is a flat out most loved for most Cricut clients and functions admirably with a fine-point sharp blade, however, what are a portion of the absolute best iron-on vinyl to utilize?

Siser Heat Transfer Vinyl – Easy to weed and they have been around for quite a while! Siser likewise has sparkle vinyl alternatives, patterned vinyl, and floral patterns just as holographic choices!

My Vinyl Direct – Vinyl Direct has much progressively then just HTV. They have a lot of examples, colors, and surfaces.

Firefly Heat Transfer Vinyl – Firefly is broadly known and confided in the brand. In addition to the fact that it has extraordinary appraisals, they have a phenomenal determination! What's more, if you are searching for extraordinary fluffy flocked vinyl or glitter vinyl they have you secured!

Fame Heat Transfer Vinyl – This brand is incredible when you are chasing for a wide choice of colors. The other advantage of this brand is that it is less expensive than a few other options if you are on a spending limit!

MAT to utilize: Generally the standard hold mat will work with all vinyl.

Adhesive Vinyl – Use Vinyl Setting

Adhesive vinyl is a nearby most loved to the HTV. There are endless uses for adhesive vinyl, for example, decals, mugs, decorations, compartments, divider craftsmanship and so forth. Here are probably the best marks beneath for AV!

There are fundamentally 2 classifications of adhesive vinyl – changeless open-air and removable indoor – with different kinds inside every category. Vinyl will consistently be explained as one of those sorts and you should utilize in like manner to the undertaking for best outcomes.

For instance, removable adhesive vinyl would work extraordinary as a removable wall decal while lasting vinyl will work better for a wood sign you intend to hold tight your front entryway.

For adhesive vinyl, you will generally utilize the vinyl setting on your Cricut.

Oracal Vinyl – This vinyl is my own top decision when I am considering starting an adhesive vinyl project. Oracal is viewed as the industry leader with regards to craft vinyl. This vinyl is intended a year ago. You can likewise discover moves of this on Vinyl Direct here in both gleaming and matte!

Cricut Adhesive Vinyl – Cricut is as yet an extraordinary go-to resource for AV. All in all, Cricut tends to be increasingly expensive BUT there are times that I locate a superior conceal in a shading I am checking for with Cricut's vinyl.

4. Happy Crafters – Honestly this is only an upbeat place site – you will discover vinyl of various kinds and numerous other art-related supplies!

Mat to utilize: Standard hold fill in also for adhesive vinyl.

Cardstock

Paper and cardstock are used to make paper flowers

1. Recollections cardstock – Recollections is a brand by Michael's craft store, however, they can likewise be discovered online! Utilize this brand the most for my paper creates.

2. Savage Universal paper rolls – I recently found how brilliant Savage paper functions for paper creating. Even though it appears to be a little expensive forthright, it endures so any longer!

3. Paper and More – Paper and more is a believed resource I have utilized and I love the more one of a kind colors they have.

4. Cards and Pockets – This site has been with me for a considerable length of time and in light of current circumstances, the color alternatives are unrivaled to most.

Thin chipboard – useful for wreaths or large letter or number patterns. Set dial to custom and select chipboard.

Thin poster board – use for projects with foundations or huge patterns. Dial ought to be set to the poster board.

Sticker paper or tattoo paper – If you are utilizing the print and cut component, consider doing it on sticker or tattoo paper for a fun project. I like to cut my own organizer stickers! Utilize the cardstock setting for these also with the fine-point blade.

Vellum – Vellum is simply one more sort of paper that is typically sensitive and translucent. It works extraordinary for any variety of paper makes. For vellum, try to set the dial to paper or vinyl.

Cellophane – Every from time to time I discover a task I am making needs an adaptable and clear like material – cellophane works incredible for that and your Cricut can cut it! Cellophane should be cut at the lightest setting, typically paper or the one speck before it.

Deep-cut blade – What Can I cut?

For every one of the materials underneath you will need to set you dial or machine to custom and search the name of the material to set the proper cut pressure.

Elastic – Want to make your very own stamps? You thoroughly can with this extraordinary elastic and the deep-cut blade.

Wood veneer embellishments – You may have the option to utilize a fine-point blade with the wood veneer if it is slim enough, however likely will need the deep blade in most cases.

Magnets – Creating your very own magnets can be extremely fun. An astounding teacher thankfulness blessing actually.

Leather – Leather is extremely popular at this moment, particularly those sweet leather earrings!

Craft foam – Foam is particularly great for children's crafts. Pre-cut a lot of fun shapes and have your children appreciate some crafty fun time!

Matboard – Matboard is a basic cardboard yet more pleasant. So any project you need to utilize cardboard for can work with the deep cut blade!

Felt sheets – Love felt blooms or crafts? At that point let your Cricut take the necessary steps for you! You can likewise do hardened felt sheets!

Glitter cardstock – I love glitter cardstock for a sort of project. I have cut it with the fine-point cutting edge yet the deep works better particularly with the chunky glitter paper.

Fabric Blade – What Can I Cut?

The fabric blade is entirely explicit to fabric and you will generally keep the fabric setting set up on the dial. Here are a couple of my preferred fabric spots to shop. You can likewise cut fabric with the 2 past blades talked about yet I suggest trying the fabric intended blade a try!

Spoonflower – If you need A LOT of fabric to pick from or to specially craft your very own fabric in a couple of short snaps then Spoonflower is the best approach!

Joann Fabrics – Many of you have most likely known about Joann's Fabrics. They have been around quite a while and some of you may have a store close by. If you don't, you can shop here online!

Fabric Direct – If you need a big website with fabric and at discount costs, at that point make certain to look at fabric direct. I have acquired velvet from them for some fall pumpkin creates and adored it!

Mat to utilize: Fabric grip mat or standard grip.

Knife Blade (Cricut Maker only) – What Can I Cut?

With the knife (Cricut Maker only) you can cut a ton of comparable Cricut materials similarly as with the deep blade BUT the thing that matters is that it can cut 2-3x thicker materials then the Explore can deal with! In fact, the knife blade can slice material up to 3mm thick! All the more significantly, it does it with an increasingly exact and clean accuracy cut then the deep cut blade with Explore.

Mat to utilize: A crisp standard grip mat will work for materials more slender then 1 mm however ordinarily the blade sharp edge is utilized on thicker materials, so I prescribe the solid grip mat. In case you're utilizing something like 3 mm balsa wood you may likewise need to utilize some painter's tape around the edges to ensure it doesn't slide mid-cut.

Settings: For the wood, chipboard, and leather there are settings you can choose with you click on "see all materials" in Design Space. Craft foam typically functions admirably on the thicker cardstock setting.

Rotary Blade (Cricut Maker only) – What Can I cut?

Washi Sheets – Washi Sheets are amazing specialty papers. Typically they have a fabulous time surfaces or prints on them. They work delightfully for cards!

Crepe paper – Can you say simple crepe paper blossoms?

Cork – Cork can be sensitive to cut so the revolving blade is perfect!

Tissue paper – Cut tissue paper with as well! Make a point to pick a greater paper like the one connected here.

Delicate fabrics – Fabrics that are progressively fragile like tulle, organza, and lace are a solid match for the rotary blade.

Mat to utilize: You can utilize a fabric grip mat for light fabrics and cork; however, utilize a standard or light hold tangle for crepe and light for tissue paper.

Settings: Delicate fabrics ought to be set to the fabric selection setting, while the tissue, crepe, and washi paper ought to be put on their named setting inside custom settings.

CHAPTER 7:

Selling and Make Money

In terms of making money from the comfort of your home, you easily achieve that with a Cricut machine. However, you have to bear in mind that there are a number of competitors out there, thus you have to put in extra efforts in order to stand a chance to succeed.

For you to become successful in the Cricut world of crafts, you have to keep the following in mind;

1. Dare to be different

You have to be yourself, unleash your quirkiness and creativity.

Those that have been in the Cricut crafts world for some time know all about the knockout name tiles. They became a hit and in no time, everyone was producing and selling them.

In the crafting world, that is the norm. Thus, you could be among the earliest people to jump on a trend to ride the wave until the following hot seller surfaces. Mind you, that strategy of selling Cricut crafts can become costly and tiresome if you are not careful.

The basic idea here is to add your flair and personal style, and not to completely re-invent the wheel. For example, let's say you come across two name tiles on Etsy, one looks exactly like the other 200+ on sale on the site, while the second one has a few more tweaks and spins on it. The seller of the second product will possibly charge more and accrue a higher profit because his/her product is unique and stands out from the rest.

When you design your products, don't be afraid to tweak your fonts, because even the simplest of tweaks and creativity can make your product stand out from the rest.

Remember this; if you create a product that looks exactly like others, you are only putting yourself in a 'price war', where no one usually wins.

2. Keep it narrow

A lot of crafters out there believe that creating and selling everything under the sun translates into more patronage, and more money, but that isn't how it works. On the contrary, it might only result in a huge stock of unsold products, more burn out and heavy cost. Rather than producing materials here and there, you should focus on being the best in your area of craftiness, so that when people need specific products in your area, they'll come to you.

It can be very tempting to want to spread your tentacles because it might seem like the more you produce, the more options you'll provide for your clients, but that might be counterproductive.

Take out time to think about your area of strength and focus your energy on making products that you'd be known for. It is better to be known as an expert in a particular product than to be renowned for someone that produces a high number of inferior products.

Thus, you should keep it narrow and grow to become the very best in your area of craft.

3. be consistent

If you intend to become successful, you have to work on your Cricut craft business consistently. Some people work once a week or thereabout because they sell as a hobby; however, if you intend to make in-road in your business, you have to work every day.

If you have other engagements and can't work every day, then you should create a weekly schedule and stick to it. If you shun your business for weeks and months at a time, then you will not go anywhere with it.

Apart from consistency in work and production, you also have to be consistent with your product quality and pricing. When your customers are convinced about your products, they will easily recommend you to their friends, family, business partners, and many others.

In business, there are ups and downs, thus, you shouldn't reduce your work rate because things are not going as planned. Success doesn't come easy, but one of the surest ways of being and maintaining success is by consistently doing the things you love.

4. be tenacious

It is not easy to run a business because it involves a lot of hard work, sweat, and even heartbreaks. Thus, you have to bear in mind that there will be days when you will feel like throwing in the towel.

However, you have to look at the bigger picture, because the crafting business is not a get rich quick scheme. Remember, quitters never win, so quitting isn't an option. Keep doing the things you love, and keep improving. Successful people never give up. They suffer many setbacks but they don't stop.

Thus, for you to be successful in your craft, you have to be tenacious and resilient. Be willing to maneuver your way through tough times, and do not forget to pick up lessons.

5. Learn everyday

Be willing to learn from people that have been successful in the business. You don't necessarily have to unravel everything by yourself, because whatever it is you are doing, others have already done it in the past.

Whether you intend to learn how to build a successful Facebook group or how to go up the Etsy ranks, remember that people have already done all that in the past, and are giving out tricks and tips they know.

Make it a tradition to learn something new about your business every day because, at the beginning of your business, you will have to do more marketing than crafting.

When you wake up in the morning, browse through the internet, gather materials and read at your spare time, because the more you learn the better your chances of being successful. They say knowledge is power, and for you to become successful as a craftsman/woman, you have to constantly seek new knowledge in the form of tips, tricks, software upgrades, marketing, design ideas, tools, accessories, and many others.

All I am saying is that you should learn without ceasing.

6. Quality control

If you intend to grow your brand, you must prioritize the selling of high-quality products. Your motto should quality over everything.

For you to easily succeed, people should know you as someone that sells top quality products, because quality wins over quantity every day of the week.

You don't want to be known as someone that produces poor quality items because when the word spreads (and it surely will); your business will pack up.

If you focus your attention and efforts on the production of high-quality materials, you will be able to withstand competition, no matter how stiff it is.

CHAPTER 8:

Cricut Design Space Top Menu

T he top menu will only become available after you have texts typed out or a design uploaded. Thus, beginning from the left is the Undo button, used to rectify mistakes. The next button on the right is the Redo button, used to repeat and action.

The Deselect button is next, and it is used as the opposite of select. The Edit button is next and it has a dropdown menu that consists of copy or paste and flip. Next is the Size button; you can use it to change the actual size of your design or explore the bottom right of the design to use the two-way directional arrow.

Right at the bottom left of the canvas is the unlock button. This feature consists of a four-way directional arrow used to widen designs without making them taller or making them taller with making them wider.

On the menu is the rotation tool, used to rotate designs to every degree possible. The last feature on the top menu is the x and y coordinates, used to position designs on the canvas.

How to Weld

It can be a little bit daunting for a Cricut Space beginner to use the weld tool, however, when you become proficient, it'll open the doors to many more projects because it is a tool that will be used often.

The weld tool is located at the bottom right corner of Design Space, under the layers panel. Other tools close to it are; flatten, contour and slice tools.

In Cricut Design Space, the weld tool does the following;

· Connects cursive text and scrip in order for it to cut as a single word instead of individual letters

· Merge multiple layers and shapes into a single layered image

· Take of cut lines from different shapes and cut them as one big image

For you to use weld, the text or shapes you intend to weld together must be touching or overlapping each other.

To select the layers you intend to weld together; select a layer, hold down 'ctrl' and select the other layer. After selecting both layers, click 'weld'. If you intend to weld the whole layers on your canvas, click 'select all' to select all the layers and click 'weld'.

If you weld different layers together, it becomes a single image and will cut out in one color and on one mat.

Without selecting multiple layers, the weld option will not be available for use.

In order to weld texts, you have to make sure that the letters are all touching each other. Thus, you have to reduce the spacing of the letters until they begin to touch each other. Once you do this, you can select everything and click weld.

How to Slice

The slice tool is a feature in Cricut Design Space that cuts one design element out of another. You can use it to cut text from a shape, cut one shape from another shape, or cut overlapping shapes from each other. Below is an example and we will cut text out from a heart shape.

Choose a font

Use any font you prefer, but decrease your letter spacing from to 0.9 so that your letters will link together.

Weld the text

When you're done with the spacing, you have to transform your letters into a single image by using the weld tool. When you weld your letters, it permanently connects all the design elements into one image.

Choose an SVG

You can find a heart SVG from Lovesvg.com. You just need to ungroup everything and simply delete the unwanted elements.

Set the size of your design

You need to resize the image. Depending on the size you want, simply type the intended size on the width box. For this example, we'll stick to 5.5 inches.

Arrange the design

You need to arrange the text and heart, by clicking 'arrange'.

Use the slice tool

When you have arranged your design perfectly, select your text and hold down 'ctrl' key, select the heart and click 'slice'. Now, you can remove the text from the heart and delete.

iii. Once your design is done, it is time to cut vinyl.

How to flatten

The flatten tool is a feature used to turn multi-layered images into a single-layered image.

What does flatten do in Cricut Design Space?

The tool is used in the making of decals, labels, stickers, and much more. You can flatten multiple layers of SVG cut files into single layered images, before printing and cutting.

With the flatten tool, you can achieve the following;

· Remove cut lines from an image

· Transform multi-layered images into a single layered image

· Used to transfer regular images into printable images for print-and-cut

· Used to maintain distinct colors of multi-layered images

Using the flatten tool;

· To select the layers you intend to flatten together, lick 'select all' or hold down 'ctrl' and select the layers

· After selecting, click flatten at the bottom right corner

· When you do that, the image is now flattened.

How to Attach

Basically, there are two distinct reasons for using the attach tool;

· To keep scoring/writing lines in the right place

· To keep shapes in the correct place on the mat as on the canvas

Using the Attach tool to maintain the same arrangement

If you want all the pieces of your project to remain in the exact location during cutting, as it is on your CDS canvas, you have to;

· Select all the items of each color

· Click 'attach' at the lower right corner

· Repeat the process for each color layer until they are all nested under a label that says "attach'

With the attach tool, you will be able to cut out your projects exactly the way you arranged them on your Cricut canvas.

How to Group/Ungroup

Group on Cricut Design Space means to group two or more layers into one layer. On the other hand, Ungroup means breaking up a layer group into separate layers. There are different types of group layers, and if a layer is grouped multiple times, you will have to ungroup them multiple times, in order to separate them completely.

Group: To select multiple layers, you have to press 'ctrl' and select your layers on your computer. After selection, you have to click your mouse right and click the Group button. If you wish, there is also the option of creating multiple groups within groups, because it makes it easier to deal with complex designs.

In Design Space, groups work better with layers, especially when you're trying to manipulate some parts of a design. With Group, you can easily resize or stretch the selection.

Ungroup: It is very easy to ungroup designs that are grouped together. To ungroup, you need to select the layer you intend to ungroup, right click your mouse, and click on the ungroup button or select Ungroup. There are layers that might have been grouped multiple times, thus, if you intend to Ungroup completely, you have to continuously select again and again, and keep clicking Ungroup, until it's completely done.

The primary reason for using the ungroup feature is to change or manipulate some part of a design. The change could be physical, or it could be manipulating some parts of a design by welding, attaching, or using some other methods, without touching on the rest of the design

How to duplicate/delete if you intend to duplicate a layer or set of layers, you have to select the part of the design or the layers you intend to duplicate, right click your mouse and click the Duplicate button.

On the other hand, if you intend to delete a single layer or a set of layers, you have to select the part of the design or the layers you intend to delete, right click your mouse, and select the Delete button.

If you have two designs and you intend to retain only one, select the design you intend to delete, right click your mouse, and click the Delete option.

How to color sync

The reason for such result lies with the fact that you may have used several images from the images tab, all being with slightly different shades of similar colors. In order to overcome this, go up into the top right-hand corner under the green button marked 'Make It'. You will find the option 'Color Sync'. By clicking on it, you will allow the function to pull up every single item on your project to be sorted out by similar color groups.

Here is an example whereby six different shades of green emerge. Consequently, Color Sync will identify six different shades of green, making six different green cutting mats as you make your project. If the final result of your project is to have multiple shades, then there is no need to modify anything. However, if you wish to streamline in order to obtain one green cutting mat, all you have to do is to select items and drag them into different colors. By doing this, you avoid going into each individual layer through a manual change of color. On the other hand, if the purpose is to modify the color in order to obtain one shade, like for instance if you want to put together similar colors to one mat, then select the color shade bar situated on the left-hand side and pull that into the color you want to switch into. This option allows to streamline different colors of cutting mat to only a few. The choice is yours.

Using Text in Cricut Design Space

Once you sign into Cricut Design Space, select one of the three places marked with arrows to start a new project. Then click the three line icon on the top left to proceed for a 'New Project'. As you start a new project, you will be directed to a gridded design space called a Canvas. Select the left sidebar which contains the text icon. A small box will emerge, shown by a second arrow, in which you can enter your text. Once the text entered, chose a font which can be found on the far left arrow. You will quickly notice how the font has large spaces between the letters. To remedy this and bring the letters closer together modify the letter space to a smaller one (negative numbers can also be used to reach the effect needed).

Getting Started with Text

Start typing your text by simply clicking the text icon located on the left toolbar. A text box will appear in which you can start inserting your text. Font, style, and size as wells as line spacing and letter

211

spacing can be selected by going on the top toolbar. It is advisable to type your text first and then make the changes you want afterward.

How to Access Special Characters

You can access special characters by using Humble Scrip which provides many options. You can access it by typing 'character map' in your system search box. The app will appear. A drop-down menu indicates which Font you are working with. Secure the option 'Advanced View' is properly checked. Then modify the Character set to Unicode and finally group by Unicode Subrange. At this stage, a new box will appear for the Unicode Subrange. Scroll it all the way to the bottom and select 'Private Use Characters'.

CHAPTER 9:

Tips and Tricks and
Hacks for Cricut Design Space.

1. You Can Customize Make It Now Projects

When you are initial getting started in Design Space, I believe it is best to relieve in and also not attempt to discover whatever at once. Make It Now tasks are tasks that have already been designed, all you have to do is reduced.

To modify Make It Now project, clack on the image of the project you intend to make. It will open up and reveal the materials you need and also instructions. It is a wonderful starting point for your projects and you can customize them to make them your own.

2. You Can Find Even More Ready-Made

If you like the idea of projects that are presently formed, you may wish to have a look at the area in Design Space. Did you know that you can produce a profile and also share your developments? It's a reasonably brand-new attribute, but it is so agreeable to see countless other Cricut users and what they create. They work just like the Make It Now projects, yet they are made by Cricut individuals instead of Cricut themselves.

3. Filter Images

When you prepare to make your very own tasks in Design Space, you will certainly soon understand that there are lots of pictures to pick from! One way that I keep from spending every one of my crafting time scrolling via images is to filter them.

Pictures can be filtered in countless means. The first option is whether you are intending to look for pictures that remain in the cloud or ones that have actually been downloaded to your tool to make use of offline. Following off, you can filter by possession. You can pick all possessions, "my pictures", posted, totally free, Cricut Access, as well as purchased.

You can likewise look for a certain kind of image. The choices to filter by are: any kind of type, 3D appearances, things & backgrounds, boundaries, cards & envelopes, frames phrases as well as. Finally, you can pick the layer kind. You can pick any type of layer, multi-layer or single-layer

As you can picture, searching for a photo that is in the cloud, free, a border and also single-layer will certainly bring up considerably less photos that you would certainly require to browse to find the one that will certainly function just right for your task.

4. Know How to Read the Images

When looking for photos, there are a number of things you may wish to look at. If the image is encompassed in the Cricut Contact registration it will have a little eco-friendly banner and an "an" in the top left corner. Near the bottom in the left edge is the rate, or it will certainly say "bought" if you have actually currently acquired it.

To find extra information click on the "I" in the bottom best corner. A box will turn up that claims that title of the image, the ID number of the photo and the cartridge or set that it is from will be hyperlinked. You may desire to click the web link to the cartridge to see comparable images if you like the style of a picture.

5. Attach.

Among one of the most typical concerns that brand-new Design Space customers experience is when they have everything precisely where they desire them on the Design Space display, yet when they most likely to cut it jumbles every little thing up on the cutting mat.

By default, Design Space will certainly reposition the pictures to take advantage of the products you are utilizing. Then choose affix, if you desire to maintain things spaced precisely as you have them on the screen you require to select all of the photos and also.

6. Creating Fonts.

One of the most effective Design Space tips I can give you is for when you are wanting to create with your Cricut. There is a great deal of irritation when someone goes to complete their task only to see that it simply laid out the font, it didn't really load it in.

Often it is tough to picture what a typeface will look like once it is drawn. The Cricut device's task is to analysis lines, whether it is to reduce them or attract them. You will see precisely where the blade or pen will certainly go if you follow the line however. A lot of typefaces will have internal as well as external lines leaving a space that looks like it requires to be filled out.

The font you pick for composing is very crucial; so vital that Cricut has actually made particular" creating" typefaces. They are font styles that consist of only one line as well as give you the look you want when writing with your Cricut.

7. Slice Only 2 Layers.

The piece function in Design Space permits you to take 2 forms and cut one from the other. I think about it as a cookie cutter. A great deal of disappointment comes when you have actually the pictures picked; however, the piece button is grayed out and won't allow you cut.

The answer is constantly TWO! Anytime this occurs to me I understand that I somehow have more than two layers picked. Also, when I assume I do not, I look in the layers panel and also indeed, I do. Design Space will certainly never let you have more than 2 photos selected when you are slicing.

8. Weld Letters.

When dealing with typefaces, especially manuscripts, you will probably want to connect and WELD the letters.

When you move them where each letter is overlapping the other, you need to WELD. The only way to get letters to produce a single word that is reduced as one item is to overlap the letters and then WELD them.

9. Locate the font name that you used (even bonded).

In some cases, you will wish to know what the typeface is that you utilized, especially if you are returning to a task you currently developed. Design Space will inform you the font style, even if it has been changed into a photo by welding it.

Beneath the symbols at the leading there will be a tiny and it will state "See picture details". Click on that as well as a box will open up that will inform you the chosen typeface.

10. Contour to Hide Parts of an Image.

If there is an image that has parts in it that you don't want, you can remove them! The shape feature enables you to get rid of cut (or creating) lines from a picture.

11. Modification Project Copies # Instead of Copy as well as Paste.

There might be times you need a lot of one photo or more than one whole task cut. You can duplicate as well as paste, however honestly, the easiest means to make more than one of something is to make use of the "project copies" feature instead.

As soon as you have your photo or job ready, proceed as well as send it to cut. In the leading left edge, you can enter in the amount of the job you want and it will instantly place that number on the cutting floor covering.

12. Move as well as Hide Images on Cutting Screen.

In some cases, relocating a cut will assist you conserve much more materials, or you may want to conceal a picture so it won't reduce. Once you get to the cut display, you can rearrange images, move them from one floor covering to another and even conceal them.

Hacks

Wash Your Mats with Soap, Water, and a Gentle Scrubber

Because Cricut strongly encourages you not to clean your mats, it's imperative that you know you're doing this at your own risk. A large number of Cricut craftsmen, however, have said that this little trick has saved them at least for a couple of weeks from having to buy a new mat.

Because Cricut doesn't support any efforts to boost the enduring grip strength on their mats, it's best to stop trying this hack until you're sure you'd need a new mat anyway, so if it doesn't perform well, you can get a new one without feeling like you've lost something.

You can gently clean the adhesive grip side of your mat using warm water (don't go too hot or you might melt the adhesive on your mat) and a mild dish soap like Dawn, Fairy, or Palmolive, and the soft side of a kitchen sponge.

This will ensures that you can use most of the features of the Cricut Design Space. Follow these simple steps and take a look at this selection to clean it well . Then, below, take a look at the best free fonts for Cricut that we have. Make sure you have a Cricut Access membership, and then follow the following steps.

Use Non-Alcohol Wipes to Clean your Mats

Because Cricut strongly encourages you not to clean your mats, it's imperative that you know you're doing this at your own risk. Nonetheless, this hack has been tested by a decent number of people and found it to be a perfect way to give their mats a few extra weeks of life. This is a fundamental step.

Using baby wipes or non-alcohol wipes on your mats can loosen stuff that's caught in your mat's grip, clear away dirt or paper leaves, and can give you a few extra weeks of grip power in your mats!

Don't add too much pressure if you don't want to ground debris any further in, or even scrape the adhesive completely off the surface.

Rinse the mat and pat dry thoroughly with a linen dish towel or a high-quality paper towel that does not leave any residue behind. Schedule the mat to dry completely for an hour or two after you have done so, and then give it a shot to see how much the wash has helped you out.

Doing all these hacks over time should give you an idea of what works, what doesn't, and how much you need to swap your Cricut mats.

Clean your Blades

You can find that your blades are snagging on your materials after some period of continuous use, or that the cuts aren't as sharp as you would light them up to be. If this is the case, remove the housing from its attachment clamp and push the button at the top of the housing. It will stretch the blade beyond the casing, but will also give you a comfortable grip on the blade while you clean it up. Highest priority on the rundown.

CHAPTER 10:

Cricut Design Space Vocabulary

W hen working with the Cricut cutting machines and Design Space, you are going to come across different terminology. The following is a glossary of the Cricut vocabulary to help you better understands the system. The following are general Cricut terminology as "Design Space" terminology

Backing

Backing is the back sheet of material such as vinyl. It is the part of the material that gets stuck onto the cutting mat and is usually the last part of the material to be removed after cutting, weeding, and transfer of the project.

Bleed

The bleed refers to a space around each item to be cut. This gives the cutting machine the ability to make a more precise cut. It is a small border that separates cutting items on a page. This option can be turned off, but it is not recommended.

Bonded Fabric

Bonded fabric is material that is not very elastic, it is held together with adhesive and is not typical woven type fabric.

If there is some gunk visible on the blade, pinch around the blade shaft using a very careful grip with your opposite thumb and forefinger, and bring it back, making sure you don't go against the blade angle as you do. This will remove any foreign material from your blade tip and make your cuts more accurate.

You may also take a ball of tin foil and poke the blade a few times into the cup, which will remove debris while also allowing a minor sharpening on them.

Blade

Cricut has a few different types of cutting blades and tips. Each blade has its own unique function enabling it to cut various materials.

Blade Housing

The blade housing is the cylindrical tube that holds the blade and fits into the blade head and blade accessory compartment of the Cricut cutting machine.

Blank

Cricut offers items, called blanks, to use with various projects for vinyl, iron-on, heat transfer vinyl, or infusible ink. These items include T-shirts, tote bags, coasters, and baby noisiest.

Brayer

The Brayer is a tool that looks a bit like a lint roller brush. It is used to flatten and stick material or objects down smoothly as it irons out bubbles, creases, etc.

Bright Pad

A Bright Pad is a device that looks like a tablet. This device has a strong backlight to light up materials to help with weeding and defining intricate cuts. It is a very handy tool to have and can be used for other DIY projects as well.

Butcher Paper

Butcher paper is the white paper that comes with the Cricut Infusible Inks sheets. It is used to act as a barrier between the EasyPress or iron when transferring the ink sheet onto a blank or item.

Carriage

The carriage is the bar in the Cricut cutting machine which the blade moves across.

Cartridge

Cartridges are what the older models of the Cricut cutting machine used to cut images. Each cartridge would hold a set of images. They can still be used with the Cricut Explore Air 2 which has a docking site for them. If you want to use them with a Cricut Maker you will have to buy the USB adaptor. Design Space still supports the use of Cartridge images.

Cartridges also come in a digital format.

Cricut Maker Adaptive Tool System

The Cricut Maker comes with an advanced tools system control using intricate brass gears. These new tools have been designed to aid the machine in making precise cuts and being able to cut more materials such as wood, metal, and leather.

Cut Lines

These are the lines along which the cutting machine will cut out the project's shapes.

Cutting Mat

There are a few different types of cutting mats also known as machine mats. Most of the large mats can be used on both the Cricut Explore Air 2 and the Cricut Maker. The Cricut Joy needs mats that are designed specifically for it.

Cut Screen

When you are creating projects in Design Space, there is a green button on the top right-hand corner of the screen called the Make it button. When the project is ready to be cut, this button is clicked on. Once that button has been clicked, the user is taken to another screen where they will see how the project is going to be cut out. This is the Cut Screen.

Drive Housing

The Drive Housing is different from the Blade Housing in that it has a gold wheel at the top of the blade. These blades can only be used with the Cricut Maker cutting machine.

EasyPress

A Cricut EasyPress is a handheld pressing iron that is used for iron-on, heat transfer vinyl (HTV), and infusible ink. The EasyPress' latest models are the EasyPress 2 and the EasyPress Mini.

EasyPress Mat

There are a few different EasyPress Mat sizes that are available on the market. These mats make transferring iron-on, heat transfer vinyl, and infusible ink a lot simpler. These mats should be used for these applications instead of an ironing board to ensure the project's success.

Firmware

Firmware is a software patch, update, or new added functionality for a device. For cutting machines it would be new driver's updates, cutting functionality, and so on.

Both Design Space software, Cricut cutting machines, and Cricut EasyPress 2 machines need to have their Firmware updated on a regular basis.

Go Button

This can also be called the "Cut" button. This is the button on the Cricut cutting or EasyPress machine that has the green Cricut "C" on it. It is the button that is pressed when a project is ready to be cut or pressed for the EasyPress models.

JPG File

A JPG file is a common form of digital image. These image files can be uploaded for use with a Design Space project.

Kiss Cut

When the cutting machine cuts through the material but not the material backing sheet it is called a Kiss Cut.

Libraries

Libraries are lists of images, fonts, or projects that have been uploaded by the user or maintained by Cricut Design Space.

PNG File

A PNG file is another form of a graphics (image) file. It is most commonly used in Web-based graphics for line drawings, small graphic/icon images, and text.

Ready to Make Projects

Design Space contains ready to make projects which are projects that have already been designed. All the user has to do is choose the project to load in Design Space, get the material ready, and then make it to cut the design out. These projects can be customized as well.

Scraper Tool

The Scraper tool comes in small and large. It is used to make sure material sticks firmly to a cutting mat, object, or transfer sheet.

Self-Healing Mat

Cricut has many handy accessories and tools to help with a person's crafting. One of these handy tools is the Self-Healing Mat. This mat is not for use in a cutting machine but can be used with handheld slicing tools to cut material to exact specifications

SVG File

The SVG file format is the most common format for graphic files in Cricut Design Space. This is because these files can be manipulated without losing their quality.

Transfer Sheet/Paper

A transfer sheet or transfer paper is a sheet that is usually clear and has a sticky side. These sheets are used to transfer various materials like transfer vinyl, sticker sheets, and so on onto an item.

Weeding/Reverse Weeding

Weeding is the process of removing vinyl or material from a cut pattern or design that has been left behind after removing the excess material. For example, weeding the middle of the letter "O" to leave the middle of it hollow.

Reverse Weeding would be leaving the middle of the letter "O" behind and removing the outside of it.

Weeding Tool

The Weeding tool has a small hooked head with a sharp point. This tool is used to pick off the material that is not needed on a cut. For instance, when cutting out the letter 'O' the weeding tool is used to remove the middle of the letter so that it is hollow. Cleaning up a cut design with the Weeding tool is called weeding.

CHAPTER 11:

How to Edit and Upload Images in The Cricut Machine

First, you will need to browse the image on your computer and upload it using the "Upload" command. After that, you will want to choose, from the three image options, the "Complex" type. Once you have done all that just select "Continue".

In the next part, you will be taken to a window with various editing options. You will have the option Undo/Redo any action or Zoom in/Zoom out from the image (1). On the left side you will have the most important tools for this job: "Select & erase", "Erase" and "Crop" (2). In this example, we will be using all three of these tools so you can get the full set of information from this technique. First, we will separate the basket from the rabbit and after that, we will separate the rabbit from the basket.

Step 1: If necessary zoom out to be able to view the entire picture.

Step 2: If you want to separate a small part of a larger picture, use the "Crop" tool to isolate the targeted area. In this case, we need only the basket so most of the image can be cropped out.

Step 3: Once the rest of the image is cropped we need to remove any part of the remaining picture that we don't want. To do that we can use the "Select & erase" tool.

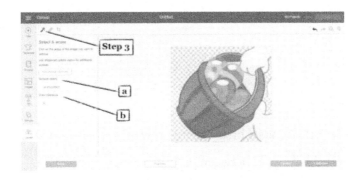

By selecting "Advanced Options" you can directly remove the color by using the "Reduce colors" tab (a). You can also increase the "Color tolerance" (b) which allows you to clear large portions more easily with the "select" method.

Step 4: To remove the fine lines and small details we can use the "Erase" tool.

Tip: Depending on your image you can increase or decrease the size of the eraser by moving the slider left or right.

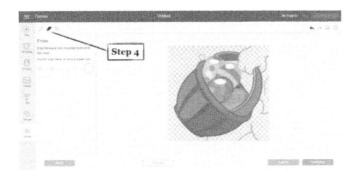

Step 5: Click "Continue" button.

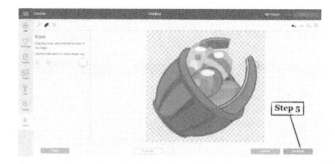

Step 6: Select the type of image that you want to save and click "Save". Here you can choose between a "Print then cut image" or "Cut image".

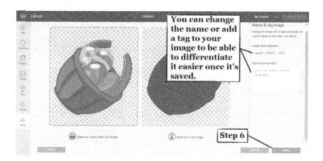

Step 7: Once we have our first part separated (the basket) we can move on to the rabbit. To do that we need to upload the image again and repeat the process.

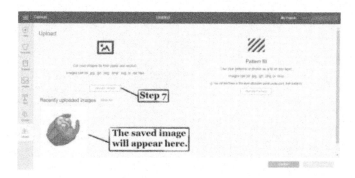

Step 8: Follow the same steps as before but now remove the basket using the "Select & erase" and the "Erase" tool again.

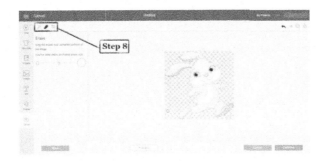

Step 9: Once the image is saved we can add our separated pictures on our canvas. To do that you have first to select each image and then use the "Insert Images" button.

Result: Each image is now considered as its own layer and can be resized, moved and edited to your liking.

Knockout Text Method

You've probably heard about this method or read about it on different forums. However, this method is only limited by your imagination and as your skills progress you will quickly realize that it can be used in multiple ways to enhance your projects.

In this example, we will use it on a text object and by the end of it, you will learn how to add a personalized twist to any text you want.

Step 1: Write your text on the canvas.

Step 2: This part is very important. Here we will edit the text in such a way that will allow the editing to be visible. You have to choose a font with thick letters. After that, you can change the spacing between the letters and the text rows. Depending on your design you might want to make sure that the letters won't touch each other. But this can vary from project to project.

Step 3: Once you are satisfied with your text you can begin adding images that will later be embedded into the final design. In this step, you can let your creativity shine. You can choose images that will be added to single letters or images that will be spread across multiple letters. Chose whatever you think fits best.

Step 4: Since the images contain multiple layers, they have to be welded together. That is why you have to select all images, except the text, and use the "Weld" tool.

Tip: Even if you add a single image, if that image contains multiple layers, it still has to be welded so you can continue with this method.

Step 5: Once the images are welded together, select both remaining objects (text and welded image) and use the "Slice" tool.

Step 6: Don't be alarmed if after the "Slice" the result will look confusing. In this part, it's best first to select the sliced text and move it to the back of the canvas. That way you will know not to delete that layer.

Step 7: All that remained now is to delete the extra objects that resulted after the "Slice".

Tip: You can use the on/off visibility option (eye symbol) for each layer to see if it actually has to be deleted or not.

Result: As you can see in the final image the flower objects are now part of the text and the extra parts have been removed from the canvas.

This was just an example to illustrate how you can learn to use the "knockout" method. It's worth mentioning that this method is extremely versatile and can be used to create a lot of different designs. Depending on your style and imagination you can adapt it and let your creativity run free.

In the next image, you can see a few more examples of this method.

Add Color to an Uploaded Image Outline

This method might seem a bit tricky at the beginning since it has a lot of steps. However, the idea is very simple, once you understand the concept you will be able to master it pretty quickly.

Step 1: Upload your image. It should have a clear and defined outline. Also, note that the more complex the image the more work you'll have to do to color each part. But more on that later.

Step 2: Select the image type as "Complex" and click "Continue".

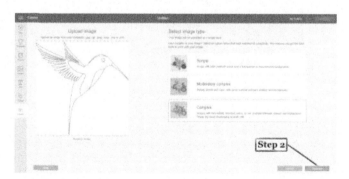

Step 3: If your image is not a .png file it will have a white background. For this method to work, you'll have to remove that background by using the "Select & erase" tool.

Step 4: Once you removed the background you should be left only with the outline of your picture.

Step 5: Select the type of the image to be and click "Continue". For this example, we saved it as a "Cut" image.

Step 6: After the image is uploaded and saved, add it to your canvas.

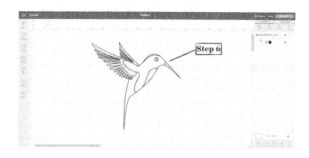

Step 7: In this step, you want to copy and paste your image. You can do that by using the combinations on your keyboard Ctrl + C and Ctrl + V. It's important not to use the duplicate function since it will not save the image in the system's memory. This will be important later on.

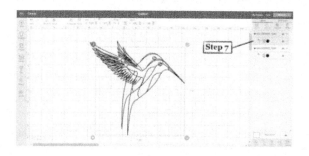

Step 8: Select both images and use the "Align" (Center) tool.

Step 9: Select the lowest image on the Layers tab and use the "Contour" tool.

Step 10: This step is very important since from this window you will be selecting the part of the image you want to fill. To make it easier, here is a strategy you can follow for this step:

1. In the bottom right corner select "Hide All Contours".

2. Click somewhere outside the outer border of your image.

This way you will be left with the inside contour you want to color.

Step 11: Select the new image, that should be the inside contour and change it to the desired color.

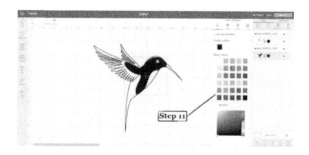

Step 12: For the method to go smoothly from here now on it's better if the images are grouped together. Therefore, you should select both images and use the "Group" command.

Step 13: If you used the Copy + Paste method, in the beginning, you can now just press Ctrl + V and paste another image outline.

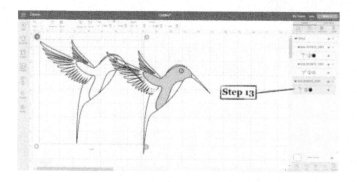

Step 14: Since our initial images are grouped they can now be easily aligned with the newly added image outline. Select the group and the new image and use the "Align" (Center) tool.

Step 15: Once the images are aligned select the lowest image on the layers tab and use the "Contour" tool again.

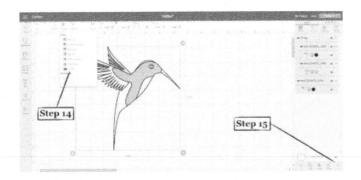

Step 16: Right now, you want to select another part of the image you want to fill. You can use the strategy from Step 10.

Step 17: Once you colored another part of the image you need to "Ungroup" the first group. That way you can avoid having a group within a group within a group later on.

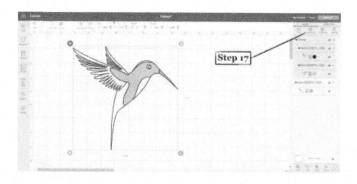

Step 18: Once all layers are ungrouped you can now use the "Group" tool on all existing layers.

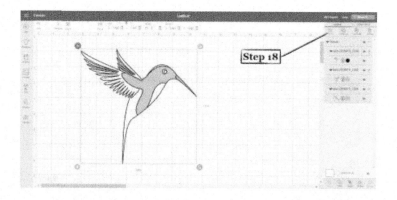

Step 19: From now on you can just repeat Steps 13-18 until you filled every part of your image.

Result: The result should be a fully colored image with a separate layer for each area.

CHAPTER 12:

Slice, Flatten, Weld, Attach and Contour Info-Graphic Slice

The slice tool is ideal for cutting out distinct forms, text, and other elements. When I chose both shapes and clicked on slice, you will see that all the original files will be cut up; to show you what the final result was, I pasted the "slice result" and then divided all the parts resulting from slicing.

Weld

The welding tool combines two or more forms in one. When I have clicked on Weld and chosen both shapes, you can see I formed a new shape. The back layer determines the color, so the original shape is pink in color.

Attach

Attach operates like grouping layers, but firm. When I have chosen both forms and clicked on attach, you will see the layers just changed color. The forms are linked, however, and this attachment will stay in location after I send my project to be cut.

Flatten

This tool supports the Print and then Cut Fill environment; if you alter the fill from no fill to print, it only applies to one layer. However, what if you want to do various forms at the moment?

When your design is finished, pick the layers you want to print together as a whole, then click on flatten. When completing your design, pick the layers you want to print together as a whole, then click on flatten.

In such case, the element becomes a print then cut design, and that's why it no longer shows a black edge through which the blade passes.

Contour

The Contour tool enables you to conceal unwanted parts of a design and will only be allowed if a model or shape has elements that can be left out.

For this instance, I combined the initial design in one form with the weld tool; then I wrote the term contour and cut it against the new form, using the Contour tool to conceal the two letters O's inner circles and the letter R's inner part.

Color Sync

Color Sync is the last panel choice.

Every color on your canvas is a different material color. If your structure has various colors of yellows or blues, do you need them? If you only need one yellow shade, like this instance. Just click and drag the tone to get rid of and drop it on the one you want to maintain.

Cricut Design Space Canvas Area

Canvas Area

There you see all your designs and elements. It's intuitive and user-friendly.

a. Canvas Grid and measurements

The area of the canvas is separated by a grid; this is good because every little square you see on the grid helps visualize the cutting mat. Ultimately, this helps maximize your room. You can alter the readings from cm to inches by clicking the top panel toggle and then selecting Settings. A window will open with all choices.

Design Space Settings

Turning off-grid and turning off-grid and

b. Selection whenever you select one or more layers, the choice is blue and can be modified from all four angles.

The "redx" deletes the layers. The upper right hand corner allows you to rotate the picture (if you need a particular angle, I suggest using the editing menu tool). The selection's reduced right button, "the tiny lock," keeps size proportional when increasing or decreasing your layer size. By clicking, you can now have distinct proportions.

c. Last but not least, zoom in and out. If you want to see in a smaller or larger scale without modifying the original size of your designs, then you can do it by pressing"+ and-" signs on the canvas' lower-left corner. That's it— you're no longer a beginner.

Conclusion

Thank you for reading this manuscript. The following step is to utilize your new found wisdom on the cutting edge craft project designing and creation offered by "Cricut". You are now poised to follow the detailed instructions described in this manuscript to create your own personalized and one of a kind craft projects that reflect your creativity and serve as an exhibit of yourself expression.The possibilities that the Cricut machine has to offer are endless. Every craftsman, beginner, or professional creates beautiful craft pieces according to their level of expertise regarding the Cricut Machine, and after reading this manuscript, you will not be left out. This manuscript has deliberated enough information that you are already ready to go and perform a great artwork of which the world will be proud. So get to work straight away and start creating beautiful crafts. Owning this type of machine is a prime opportunity for many people to develop their expertise in craftsmanship, and it's incredible if you want to venture out and try new things as a crafter because you can add so many new items to your portfolio.

As a result, this machine can literally offer never-ending opportunities for a crafter. In this manuscript, we've discussed how to set up your Cricut machine as well as the advantages of owning one, and we gave you all the information you need to be able to use it efficiently and effectively. It is very typical to get overwhelmed when you own a

Cricut machine because of all the information. Still, we told you exactly what you need to know to get started and start creating impressive and innovative projects. There's so much information out there, and the best part is that most of it is free, which means you have more opportunities to get images and things you need to craft, but it also means you get a much bigger chance to get ideas for your projects. Most people don't even know where to get information about their machine or the items they can use to start crafting, but this manuscript has all the information you need from describing the Cricut machine's most basic function to reflecting ideas for experienced users. We have also shown you that once you have the required skills and the right resources, you can cut even more with the Cricut machines, so you are aware of this as well. In this way, we've made sure you can never forget exactly what you can cut using this machine. However, if you're ever confused, there's a whole part in this manuscript on how to set up your machine and how to set up your design space. We have also included some helpful hints and tips to make sure you have some great ideas on how to make it easier for you to use this machine and the supplies, and you can use all of these tips to your advantage. If you follow the tips you've found in this manuscript, you're going to be able to find supplies easier, keep your mats cleaner, use your machine way better, maintain your machine considerably better, and even gain some amazing storage tips and actually make your craft space a place you can be proud of and feel happy and content while you're working. The ability to do that will help boost both your craftsmanship and your emotions.

CRICUT PROJECT

IDEAS:

How to Create Wonderful Objects Using your Cricut
Machine. A Step-by-Step Guide to Beginners and
Advanced Amazing Projects; Including Practical
Examples, Tips & Tricks.

JADE PAPER

256

Table Of Contents

Introduction

Are you out of ideas, and you don't have enough creativity to create your own design, image, or project? Don't worry! Just find a project you like, grab your supplies, and go for it. If you want to view all Ready-to-Make projects, you will need to access the Projects page of Cricut Design Space and scroll down to see as many projects as you want. There are a few hundreds of them, but the list is refreshed with new projects quite often (so you better keep an eye on it).

If you are using a desktop computer, or a laptop you can select a Project Category from the drop-down menu located on the upper side of the screen, or if you know what you want, you can type what you need in the search bar.

The view is a bit different if you are using the Mobile App of Design Space. From the Home view, you will see the Categories drop-down, you can tap on it to see different categories, or the Search bar to find what you need.

Have you ever wondered what happens if you click on a Ready-to-Make project? Let's say that you want to use a specific project, which comes included with the Cricut Access subscription. If you click (or tap) on it, the Project Preview window will show up, where you will see all the details you need for the project, information like:

-     Project Name

-     Difficulty Level

-     Estimated Completion Time

-     Materials Required

-     Instructions

When you want to use a project which is not included with your subscription plan, you will have the cost of the project as well. It's just like a recipe for a meal you want to cook.

Then, you can only have two options in Design Space:

1. "Make it" - if you want to leave the project as it is, and go straight to the mat preview screen;

2. "Customize" - if you want to add a personal touch to your project, as this option will take you to the design screen. You can "play" with the image size (or color), adjust it as you like, or add an extra image, then "Save" the project in your account. When you are finished customizing the project, click "Make It."

How to Make Your Own Projects

You will be able to open the projects in your Canvas view, or you can create a brand new one from scratch (by clicking on the new button from the Home screen). This is where you can play with the available options, as you can go to images and search for the image you want to use for your project. You will see the image opening in the Canvas view, and then you will have above the Edit Bar. You will get to Undo or Redo, your changes, Edit, Arrange, Flip, or rotate the object you opened in this view.

If you want to add text to it, click the Text icon, and you will see the Text Bar appearing below the Edit Bar. There you can play with the options. At any point in the editing process, you will be able to see the Make It button on the top right corner of the screen. When you are finished, click it and prepare your machine for the cut: turn it on, load the mat and place the material on it. To save material, you can consolidate color on your images, as fewer colors mean fewer materials.

Practical Examples of Projects

The Cricut world is full of project ideas you can try on your Cricut machine, and the Cricut Community looks like an endless inspiration page for all the Cricut enthusiasts out there. A very popular process you can try with your Cricut machine is the HTV (Heat Transfer Vinyl). In other words, you can create your very own custom T-shirts or the most adorable baby bodysuits. Why buy custom T-shirts when you can create your own? What you need for this project:

- A Cricut machine (from the Explore Family, or the Cricut Maker itself)

- The Cricut Iron-On Vinyl (as material)

- A simple T-shirt or baby bodysuit

262

- A Grip Mat (Green, or Light Blue)

- A Weeding tool

- A Teflon Iron

- Piece of fabric of 9" x 9," to act as a buffer between the iron and the fabric

- Files from the Cricut Access subscription plan

Another very practical project idea is a paper flower decoration in a shadow box. For this project, you will need the Cricut Maker, the StandardGrip Mat, glue, tweezers, buttons, straight pins, cardstock in multiple colors, beads, a shadow box of 9" x 9", and other baubles. This project has an intermediate level difficulty and should be done in two to three hours.

There are plenty of decorations you can make using these machines, whether it's for Christmas, Halloween, or other seasonal-themed decorations. Perhaps you are looking for something more permanent, like unique hanging planters. For this one, you will need any Cricut Explore Air or Maker, a deep cut blade, a standard grip mat, chipboard, foam brushes, a glue gun, DecoArt Acrylic parin, grey sky and sea glass, light masking tape and leather cording. Plus, you will need a plant (artificial one is better in this case), and a wire (but this is optional). If you choose the live plant, you will need a plastic recipient for soil and some small white gravel.

Choose your materials, and Design Space will help by suggesting the right tools (like blades and pens) for the job. When prompted, you should load your mat and tools, and it is taken up from there by the machine. When it is done, remove your cuts from the mats carefully, and assembly.

Just starting out can be stressful. It's good to set a goal to learn one new skill in your Cricut journey. Practice makes perfect so keep practicing till you are a pro.

Design Space is cloud-based, which means that you can design from the comfort of anywhere, save it to the cloud and still be able to access it at another location, not necessarily from your personal computer. You can begin a project on a device and end it with another without breaking stride. You can even download entire projects on your device to use offline, for the times when the Internet access is unavailable. The fun part with project ideas is that what is trending today, may be already outdated tomorrow.

CHAPTER 1:

Cricut Machine, Tools and Accessories

There are a variety of tools that can be purchased to compliment the Cricut. No matter the model that fits your lifestyle. Thankfully Cricut has compiled most of the essential tools into convenient sets. Either to start off first-time Cricut users with the necessities or for special projects, like crafting and sewing.

If purchasing a toolset is not the path you wish to take, the tools can be bought separately. In addition, there are other tools that can be bought that are not in a kit. Below is a list of kits and tools with a short explanation of their various purposes.

Tool Kits

Basic Tool Kit

All the 5 essential tools in one package;

- Scraper to clean and polish

- Spatula to lift

- Micro-tip scissors

- Weeder for vinyl

- Tweezers

Basics Starter Tool Kit

Another set of essential tools including;

- Scraper and spatula

- Point pens in metallic

- Scoring stylus

- Deep Cut Housing and 1 blade

Essential Tool Kit

Made for Cricut Explore models, this 7-piece set includes;

- Trimmer and replacement blade

- Scoring stylus

- Scraper for cleaning and polishing

- Spatula

- Micro-blade scissors

- Weeder

- Tweezers

Paper Crafting Tool Kit

This 4-piece set is perfect for professional paper crafting and includes;

- Craft mat

- Distresser for edges

- Quilling tool for spirals

- Piercer for small piece placement

Sewing Tool Kit

Sewing essentials are all in one place. This set includes;

- Thimble made of leather

- Measuring tape

- Pins and pin cushion

- Seam ripper

- Thread snips

- Fabric shears

Weeding Tool Kit

A set of 5 tools for elaborate cutting and vinyl DIY crafts includes;

- Hook tweezers

- Fine tweezers

- Hook weeder

- Weeder

- Piercer

Complete Starter Tool Kit

Perfect for the beginning Cricut user, this set includes;

- Black window cling
- Cutting mat
- Point pens in metallic
- Scoring stylus
- Deep Cut Housing and 1 Blade
- Scraper to clean and polish
- Spatula to lift
- Micro-tip scissors
- Weeder to remove negatives
- Tweezers

Single Tools

XL Scraper

Clean mats quickly and easily or adhere sizeable projects to an assortment of surfaces with this tool. Great for vinyl and can be used with all Circuit models.

Portable Trimmer

Precision cutting is achieved with the 12-inch swinging arm, and the storage for a replacement blade makes this an extra-functional tool.

Swiftly insert materials, cut, and measure from both directions with the dual-hinged rails.

Scoring Stylus.

3-dimensional projects, boxes, card, and envelopes' lines can be scored in 1 step with this tool that holds the blade for cutting and the stylus. This tool is best for Cricut Maker and Explorer models.

Applicator and Remover

Remove or apply textiles easily and make the cutting mat last longer with these functional tools. Ideal for the Cricut Maker, these tools are sold together to make working with fabric that much easier (applicator is also known as a brayer).

Scraper and Spatula

Lift and clean easily with these two tools. Made especially for the cutting mat for all sorts of projects.

Scissors

Make clean cuts with micro-tip scissors, and store them safely with the included end cap and cover for the blades (you can use a medical scissor too).

Tweezers

Secure project pieces after lifting them with the reverse-grip of this tool. Perfect to use for little items like small cuts and intricate trimmings.

Weeders

Use this tool to remove small cuts and for separating iron-on pieces and vinyl from their liners.

Accessories

Similar to the tools available for the Cricut, there are also a variety of accessories that can be purchased to compliment whatever model of Cricut you choose. Below is a list that highlights some of the available accessories and their functions. Consider purchasing them individually or take advantage of the different bundles and sets offered.

Functional Support Accessories

Specially designed accessories are made to enhance the experience of using a Cricut machine with function and style.

Mats

- Light grip

- Standard grip

- Strong grip

- Fabric grip

Scoring and Blades

- Rotary blade

- Fabric blade- bonded

- Deep cut blade

- Fine-point blade

- Premium blade made of German carbide

- Scoring stylus

Pens

- Variety of colored pens

- Extra fine tip colored pens

- Ultimate fine tip colored pens

- Fabric pen that is washable

- Variety of colored markers

Tape

- Glitter tape

Adapters and Tech

- Cartridge adapter

- Pen adapter

- Bluetooth adapter

- Accessory adapter

- USB cable

- Power cord

- Keyboard overlay

For the crafter on the go or in need of stylish and functional storage, these accessories are the perfect fit.

Pouches

•Accessory pouches for tools

Totes and Bags

- Crafters shoulder bag

- Rolling crafters tote

- Machine tote

Machine Add-On's

Cricut machines can accomplish many great things, but sometimes they could use a sidekick. That's where these machines come in.

Easy Press

Achieve the iron-on results like a professional in less than a minute! Simple to use and light to carry, this accessory is the perfect for Cricut users who want t-shirt transfers to last.

Easy Press Bundles:

- Bulk

- Ultimate

- Everything

Cuttlebug

Cut or emboss almost any material on the run with this handy machine. Achieve the professional, clean cuts you want with ease.

Cuttlebug Add-on's:

- Mats

- Dies

- Materials

- Spacer plates

- Cutting mats

Bright Pad

This durable, light pad offers a soft, adjustable light to make tracing, cutting, and easier and more comfortable on the eyes.

Sets

Basic

Perfect for the Explore machines, this set includes spatula and scraper tools, a pen set, a stylus for scoring, and a deep cut blade with its housing.

Ultimate

An enhanced set of accessories for the Explore machines, this set includes black window cling, 3 different cutting mats, a pen set, a stylus for scoring, and a deep cut blade and its housing. It also includes the basic toolset which contains spatula and scraper tools, scissors with a blade cover, a weeder, and tweezers.

Cricut Access

To maximize the possibilities with the different machines, Cricut offers a service called "Access." This membership has different levels and unique benefits such as discounts and member-only access to design services. Three different Access memberships are listed below with a brief explanation of each one.

Fonts

Hundreds of fonts, some that non-members cannot access, are available in the most affordable Access membership, Fonts. It costs $5 per month. It's not a contract, meaning at any time you can cancel the membership.

Limitations include that they are only to be used with Explore and Maker machines and the fonts do not include licensed fonts, like Disney.

Standard

A more comprehensive Access membership; Standard, offers more exclusive access and benefits. Any purchase on Cricut.com and Design Space is 10% off, and the database includes over 30,000 images, many of which are not available for non-members. It also includes the same benefits as Fonts, including the ability to cancel when needed. The cost for this membership is about $8 per month.

The limitation of this membership is that it does not include many licensed cartridges, fonts, or images such as Disney, Sesame, or Sanrio Hello Kitty products. This is probably a good package to go with if you are starting out.

Premium

The most comprehensive Access membership; Premium, combines the benefits of Fonts and Standard memberships and adds on more. Additional cartridges, images, and fonts are up to 50% off in Design Space. Free shipping is also offered for orders with a total over $50. For a yearly fee of about $120 ($10 a month), it includes access to over 1,000 projects.

One limitation, like the other memberships, is that Premium does not have access to many licensed cartridges, images, and fonts and the 50% discount cannot be applied to purchase of these items. The discounts cannot be used with other promotional offers.

Cartridges

This unique feature of the Cricut allows anyone access to professional images and fonts for whatever they desire to create. Professional to novice crafters can enjoy the versatility of the cartridges easily. The range of cartridges offered fit just about any need you may have, and one cartridge offers a variety of ideas within its theme. Simply insert the cartridge into your machine and link it to your Cricut account online to use the images and fonts. Create the perfect designs for whatever occasion! You can order cartridges online too.

Some of the cartridges available are listed below.

Licensed characters and themes

- Disney

- Sanrio

- Boy Scouts

- Marvel

- Wordsworth

- Teresa Collins

Specially designed for cards

- Holiday, Birthday and Thank you cards

- Special card designs such as pop-up designs, box cards, and everyday themes

Events

- Weddings

- Birthdays

- Babies

- Graduations

- Anniversaries

Seasons

- Spring

- Summer

- Fall

- Winter

Holidays

•Christmas

•Hanukkah

•Easter

•Thanksgiving

•New Year's

•Mother's and Father's Day

Perfect for every day

- Home décor images and fonts

- Sports images and fonts

- Religious images and fonts

- Children related images and fonts such as animals, school, and toys

Special fonts

- Disney fonts

- Varsity fonts

- Holiday-themed fonts

- Themed fonts

- Non-English fonts such as American Sign Language, the Greek alphabet, and Hebrew

CHAPTER 2:

Basic Projects

A Coloring Flowering Card Page Project with Cricut

Pick your most loved cardstock hues and prepare to make a card that is hand-hued and loaded with affection. If you need to give an additional uncommon card and blessing, leave the card un-shaded and include incorporate with certain markers or watercolor pencils (I would adore those shading endowments!).

280

Tip: Keep the plan similarly as seems to be, move things around or include your very own touch… you make the structure to shading! This likewise makes an extraordinary card for Mother's day.

Materials

- Cricut Explore air 2 and Floral Coloring Card Make-it-now project

- Cricut Design Space programming

- Flower cutouts and heart accessories structured.

- 12" x 12" StandardGrip Cricut® tangle

- Cardstock and paperwhite

- Black Cricut pen (.03 or 12 PM, fine point size)

- Colored pencils and markers – discretionary

Materials to make your own shading card with your Cricut machine

Directions

Follow directions to draw and cut the blossom shading card plan in Cricut Design Space.

Fold the card along the scoreline. Shading anyway you'd like.

Fold score lines and paste side folds inside the back of an envelope.

Add confetti inside envelope, seal and send.

Recipe Stickers

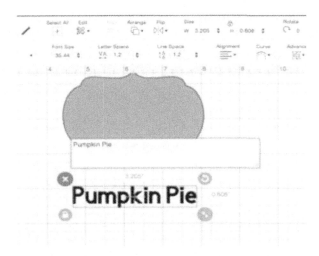

Materials needed – "Cricut Maker" or "Cricut Explore", sticker paper and cutting mat.

Step 1

Log into the "Design Space" application and click on the "New Project" button on the top right corner of the screen to view a blank canvas.

Step 2

Click on the "Images" icon on the "Design Panel" and type in "stickers" in the search bar. Click on desired image, then click on the "Insert Images" button at the bottom of the screen.

Step 3

The selected image will be displayed on the canvas and can be edited using applicable tools from the "Edit Image Bar". You can make multiple changes to the image as you need, for example, you could change the color of the image or change its size (sticker should be between 2-4 inches wide). The image selected for this project has words "stickers" inside the design, so let's delete that by first clicking on the "Ungroup" button and selecting the "Stickers" layer and clicking on the red "x" button. Click on the "Text" button and type in the name of your recipe, as shown in the picture below.

Step 4

Drag and drop the text in the middle of the design and select the entire design. Now, click on "Align" and select "Center Horizontally" and "Center Vertically".

Step 5

Select the entire design and click on "Group" icon on the top top right of the screen under "Layers panel". Now, copy and paste the designs and update the text for all your recipes.

Tip - Use your keyboard shortcut "Ctrl + C" and "Ctrl + V" to copy and paste the design.

Step 6

Click on "Save" at the top right corner of the screen to name and save your project.

Step 7

To cut your design, just click on the "Make It" button on the top right corner of the screen. Load the sticker paper to your "Cricut" machine and click "Continue" at the bottom right corner of the screen to start cutting your design.

Note – The "Continue" button will only appear after you have purchased images and fonts that are available for purchase only.

Step 8

Set your cut setting to "Vinyl" (recommended for sticker paper since it tends to be thicker than regular paper). Place the sticker paper on top of the cutting mat and follow the prompts on the screen to finish cutting your design. Viola! You have your own customized recipe stickers.

Wedding Invitations

Materials needed – "Cricut Maker" or "Cricut Explore", cutting mat and Cardstock or your choice of decorative paper/ crepe paper/ fabric, home printer (if not using "Cricut Maker").

Step 1

Log into the "Design Space" application and click on the "New Project" button on the top right corner of the screen to view a blank canvas.

Step 2

Let's customize an already existing project by clicking on the "Projects" icon on the "Design Panel" and selecting "Cards" from the "All Categories" drop-down then type in "wedding invite" in the search bar.

Step 3

For example, you could select the project shown in the picture below and click "Customize" at the bottom of the screen to edit and personalize the text of your invite.

Step 4

Click "Text" on the "Designs Panel" and type in the details of the invite. You can change the font, color and alignment of the text from the "Edit Text Bar" on top of the screen and remember to change the "Fill" to "Print" on the top of the screen.

Step 5

Select all the elements of the design and click on "Group" icon on the top right of the screen under "Layers panel". Then, click on "Save" to save your project

Step 6

Your design can now be printed and cut. Click on "Make It" button and follow the prompts on the screen first to cut the printed design.

Custom Pads

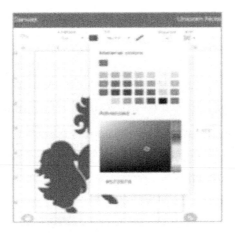

Materials needed – "Cricut Maker" or "Cricut Explore", cutting mat and washi sheets or your choice of decorative paper/ crepe paper/ fabric.

Step 1

Log into the "Design Space" application and click on the "New Project" button on the top right corner of the screen to view a blank canvas.

Step 2

Using an already existing project from the "Cricut" library and customize it. So click on the "Projects" icon on the "Design Panel" and type in "pad" in the search bar.

Step 3

Click on "Customize" so you can further edit the project to your preference. For example, the "unicorn pad" project shown below. You can click on the "Linetype Swatch" to change the color of the design.

Step 4

The design is ready to be cut. Simply click on the "Make It" button and load the washi paper sheet to your "Cricut" machine and follow the instructions on the screen to cut your project.

Crepe Paper Bouquet

Materials needed – "Cricut Maker" or "Cricut Explore", standardgrip mat, crepe paper in desired colors, floral wire, floral tape, hot glue, fern fronds and vase.

Step 1

Log into the "Design Space" application and click on the "New Project" button on the top right corner of the screen to view a blank canvas.

Step 2

Let's use an already existing project from the "Cricut" library and customize it. So click on the "Projects" icon and type in "crepe bouquet" in the search bar.

Step 3

Click on "Customize" so you can further edit the project to your preference or simply click on the "Make It" button and load the crepe paper to your "Cricut" machine and follow the instructions on the screen to cut your project.

Step 4

To assemble the design, follow the assembly instructions provided under the "Assemble" unit of the project details.

Southwest Cacti

Desert flora plants appear to be the structure extra nowadays, yet imagine a scenario in which your home doesn't get full daylight. Make your own large paper desert plants to bring home a touch of

Southwest style. These three-dimensional models can be set into basic earthenware pots, painted to coordinate your own stylistic layout. Reward: no untidy earth to manage!

Here, as well, are four straightforward structures that we slice with vinyl to tweak smooth stone liners. Include your own imaginative touch by finding various approaches to utilize these adorable prickly plant layouts.

MATERIALS and TOOLS:

- PAPER

- Art paper or enormous card stock paper

- banner board

- low-temp heated glue firearm

- paper twisting device

- shower mount or paste

- 12 × 24-inch cutting mat

- painted pot

- cutting-machine vinyl

- vinyl move material

- scissors

- weeding device

- shining device

- liners

1. Cut pieces from card stock and one bit of base from banner board.

2. Overlap enormous bits of prickly plants along score lines.

3. With twisting device, delicately shape two layers of petals of prickly plants blossom.

4. With low-temp craft glue firearm, place spot on back of one petal layer and secure it onto focal point of second petal layer with the two sets twisting upwards.

5. Use splash mount or paste to append banner board and card stock base.

6. Slide tabs of huge desert plants piece into cuts on base, leaving two base cuts in the middle.

7. Rehash with second coordinating piece.

8. Slide thefollowing piece with cut at base over other two.

9. Press tab into base on right side.

10. Rehash with conclusive tab to frame assemblage of prickly plant.

11. Add heated glue to definite little top-cut piece.

12. Join little top-cut piece to top of desert flora.

13. Slide different pieces into cut and paste set up.

14. Paste blossom to top of prickly plant.

15. Spot into painted pot

Leaf Banner

Materials needed – "Cricut Maker" or "Cricut Explore", standardgrip mat, watercolor paper and paint, felt balls, needle and thread, hot glue.

Step 1

Log into the "Design Space" application and click on the "New Project" button on the top right corner of the screen to view a blank canvas.

Step 2

Let's use an already existing project from the "Cricut" library and customize it. So click on the "Projects" icon and type in "leaf banner" in the search bar.

Step 3

Click on "Customize" so you can further edit the project to your preference or simply click on the "Make It" button and load the watercolor paper to your "Cricut" machine and follow the instructions on the screen to cut your project.

Step 4

Use watercolors to paint the leaves and let them dry completely. Then create a garland using the needle and thread through the felt balls and sticking the leaves to the garland with hot glue, as shown in the picture below.

Paper Pinwheels

Materials needed – "Cricut Maker" or "Cricut Explore", standardgrip mat, patterned cardstock in desired colors, embellishments, paper straws, hot glue.

Step 1

Log into the "Design Space" application and click on the "New Project" button on the top right corner of the screen to view a blank canvas.

292

Step 2

Let's use an already existing project from the "Cricut" library and customize it. So click on the "Projects" icon and type in "paper pinwheel" in the search bar.

Step 3

Click on "Customize" to edit the project to your preference further or simply click on the "Make It" button and load the cardstock to your "Cricut" machine and follow the instructions on the screen to cut your project.

Step 4

Using hot glue, adhere the pinwheels together to the paper straws and the embellishment, as shown in the picture below.

CHAPTER 3:

Medium Projects

Perpetual Calendar

Woodblock calendars are a cute addition to any décor. Many teachers use them on their desks, or they fit in anywhere in your home. You can find unfinished block calendars online or at most craft stores. They'll usually have two wooden cubes for the numbers, two longer blocks for the months, and a stand to hold them. Painting the wood will give you the color of your choice, but you could also stain it or look around for calendars made of different types of wood. You can use the Cricut Explore One, Cricut Explore Air 2, or Cricut Maker for this project.

Supplies Needed

Unfinished woodblock calendar

Acrylic paint in color(s) of your choosing.

Vinyl color(s) of your choosing

Vinyl transfer tape

Cutting mat

Weeding tool or pick

Mod Podge

Instructions

Paint the woodblock calendar in the colors you'd like and set aside to dry.

Open Cricut Design Space, and create a new project.

Create a square the correct size for the four blocks.

Select the "Text" button in the lower left-hand corner.

Choose your favorite font, and type the following numbers as well as all of the months: 0, 0, 1, 1, 2, 2, 3, 4, 5, 6, 7, 8

Place your vinyl on the cutting mat.

Send the design to your Cricut.

Use a weeding tool or pick to remove the excess vinyl from the text.

Apply transfer tape to each separate number and the months.

Remove the paper backing from the tape, and apply the numbers as follows.

0 and 5 on the top and bottom of the first block

1, 2, 3, 4 around the sides of the first block

0 and 8 on the top and bottom of the second block

1, 2, 6, 7 around the sides of the second block

Remove the paper backing from the tape on the months, and apply them to the long blocks, the first six months on one and the second six months on the other.

Rub the tape to transfer the vinyl to the wood, making sure there are no bubbles. Carefully peel the tape away.

Seal everything with a coat of Mod Podge.

Arrange your calendar to display today's date, and enjoy it year after year!

Wooden Gift Tags

Dress up your gifts with special wooden tags! Balsa wood is light and easy to cut. The wood tags with gold names will give all of your gifts a shabby chic charm. Change up the color of the vinyl as you see fit; you can even use different colors for different gift recipients. People will be able to keep these tags and use them for something else, as well. An alternative to balsa wood is chipboard, though it won't have the same look. The Cricut Maker is the best choice for this project, though the Cricut Explore One and Cricut Explore Air 2 can get by using the Deep Cut Blade.

Supplies Needed

Balsa wood

Gold vinyl

Vinyl transfer tape

Cutting mat

Weeding tool or pick

Instructions

Secure your small balsa wood pieces to the cutting mat, then tape the edges with masking tape for additional strength.

Open Cricut Design Space and create a new project.

Select the shape you would like for your tags and set the Cricut to cut wood, then send the design to the Cricut.

Remove your wood tags from the Cricut and remove any excess wood.

In Cricut Design Space, select the "Text" button in the lower left-hand corner.

Choose your favorite font, and type the names you want to place on your gift tags.

Place your vinyl on the cutting mat.

Send the design to your Cricut.

Use a weeding tool or pick to remove the excess vinyl from the text.

Apply transfer tape to the quote.

Remove the paper backing from the tape.

Place the names on the wood tags.

Rub the tape to transfer the vinyl to the wood, making sure there are no bubbles. Carefully peel the tape away.

Thread twine or string through the holes, and decorate your gifts!

Pet Mug

Show your love for your pet every morning when you have your coffee! A cute silhouette of a cat or dog with some paw prints is a simple but classy design. You're not limited to those two animals, either. Use a bird with bird footprints, a fish with water drops, or whatever pet you might have! You can add your pet's name or a quote to the design as well. You have the freedom here to arrange the aspects of the design however you'd like. You could put the animal in the center surrounded by the paw prints, scatter the prints all around the mug, place the animalfollowing to its name and paw prints along the top, or whatever else you can imagine. Think of this as a tribute to your favorite pet or dedication to your favorite animal, and decorate accordingly. You can use the Cricut Explore One, Cricut Explore Air 2, or Cricut Maker for this project.

Supplies Needed

Plain white mug

Glitter vinyl

Vinyl transfer tape

Cutting mat

Weeding tool or pick

Instructions

Open Cricut Design Space and create a new project.

Select the "Image" button in the lower left-hand corner and search for "cat," "dog," or any other pet of your choice.

Choose your favorite image and click "Insert."

Search images again for paw prints, and insert into your design.

Arrange the pet and paw prints how you'd like them on the mug.

Place your vinyl on the cutting mat.

Send the design to your Cricut.

Use a weeding tool or pick to remove the excess vinyl from the design.

Apply transfer tape to the design.

Remove the paper backing, and apply the design to the mug.

Rub the tape to transfer the vinyl to the mug, making sure there are no bubbles. Carefully peel the tape away.

Enjoy your custom pet mug!

Organized Toy Bins

How much of a mess is your kids' room? We already know the answer to that. Grab some plastic bins and label them with different toy categories, and teach your child to sort! You can use the type of bins that suit your child or their room best. Many people like to use the ones that look like giant buckets with handles on the sides. There are also more simple square ones. You could even use cheaper laundry baskets or plastic totes with or without the lids. Once your child is old enough to read the labels, it will be easier for them to put away toys and find them again to play. You can add images to the designs as well—whatever will make your child like them best! You can use the Cricut Explore One, Cricut Explore Air 2, or Cricut Maker for this project.

Supplies Needed

Plastic toy bins in colors of your choice

White vinyl

Vinyl transfer tape

Cutting mat

Weeding tool or pick

Instructions

Open Cricut Design Space and create a new project.

Select the "Text" button in the lower left-hand corner.

Choose your favorite font and type the labels for each toy bin. See below for some possibilities.

Legos

Dolls

Cars

Stuffed animals

Outside Toys

Place your vinyl on the cutting mat.

Send the design to your Cricut.

Use a weeding tool or pick to remove the excess vinyl from the text.

Apply transfer tape to the words.

Remove the paper backing and apply the design to the bin.

Rub the tape to transfer the vinyl to the bin, making sure there are no bubbles. Carefully peel the tape away.

Organize your kid's toys in your new bins!

Froggy Rain Gear

Kids love to play outside in the rain. It can be hard to get them to dress properly for it, though. Decorate a raincoat and rain boots with a cute froggy design that will have them asking to wear them! A simple raincoat and boots that you can find at any store for a reasonable price become custom pieces with this project. The outdoor vinyl is made to withstand the elements and last for ages. You can customize this even more by adding your child's name or change up the theme completely with different images. You can use the Cricut Explore One, Cricut Explore Air 2, or Cricut Maker for this project.

Supplies Needed

Matching green raincoat and rain boots

White outdoor vinyl

Vinyl transfer tape

Cutting mat

Weeding tool or pick

Instructions

Open Cricut Design Space and create a new project.

Select the "Image" button in the lower left-hand corner and search for "frog."

Choose your favorite frog and click "Insert."

Copy the frog and resize. You will need three frogs, a larger one for the coat and two smaller ones for each boot.

Place your vinyl on the cutting mat.

Send the design to your Cricut.

Use a weeding tool or pick to remove the excess vinyl from the design.

Apply transfer tape to the design.

Remove the paper backing and apply the design to the coat or boot.

Rub the tape to transfer the vinyl to the rain gear, making sure there are no bubbles. Carefully peel the tape away.

Dress your kid up to play in the rain!

Snowy Wreath

Wreaths are a popular decoration year-round. This one is perfect for winter. You can buy premade grapevine wreaths at almost any store, or you can get really crafty and assemble one yourself. The berry stems can be found in the floral units of craft stores. Silver will fit the snowy theme well, but you could also use red for a holiday-themed look or an entirely different color. You can also change up the whole project to theme it toward your winter holiday of choice. You can use the Cricut Explore One, Cricut Explore Air 2, or Cricut Maker for this project.

Supplies Needed

Grapevine wreath

Silver berry stems

Spray adhesive

Silver and white glitter

Piece of wood to fit across the center of the wreath

Wood stain, if desired

Drill and a small bit

Twine

White vinyl

Vinyl transfer tape

Cutting mat

Weeding tool or pick

Instructions

Thread the silver berry stems throughout the grapevine wreath.

Use the spray adhesive and glitter to create patches of "snow" on the wreath.

If you want to stain your wood, do so now and set it aside to dry.

Open Cricut Design Space and create a new project.

Select the "Text" button in the lower left-hand corner.

Choose your favorite font and type, "Let it snow."

Place your vinyl on the cutting mat.

Send the design to your Cricut.

Use a weeding tool or pick to remove the excess vinyl from the text.

Apply transfer tape to the words.

Remove the paper backing and apply the design to the wood piece.

Rub the tape to transfer the vinyl to the wood, making sure there are no bubbles. Carefully peel the tape away.

Drill two small holes in the corner of the wood and thread the twine through.

Hang your wreath and sign for the winter season!

CHAPTER 4:

Advanced Projects

Felt Roses

MATERIALS NEEDED:

SVG files with 3D flower design

Felt Sheets

Fabric Grip Mat

Glue Gun

- STEPS:

- First of all, upload your Flower SVG Graphics into the Cricut design space as explained in the "Tips" unit. ("How to import images into Cricut Design Space)

- Having placed the image in the project, select it, right-click and click "Ungroup". This allows you to resize each flower independent of the others. Since you are using felt, it is recommended that each of the flowers are at least 6 inches in size.

- Create several copies of the flowers, as many as you wish, selecting the colors you want in the Color Sync Panel (by dragging and dropping the images on to the color you would want them to be cut on). Immediately you're through with that, click on "Make it" on the Cricut design space.

- Click on "Continue". After your Cricut Maker is connected and registered, under the "materials" options, select "Felt".

- If your rotary blade is not in the machine, insert it.following, on the Fabric Grip Mat, place the first felt sheet (in order of color), then, load them into your Cricut Maker. Press the "cut" button when this is done.

- After they are cut, begin to roll the cut flowers one by one. Do this from the outside in. Make sure that you do not roll them too tight. Use the picture as a guide.

- Apply Hot Glue on the circle right in the middle and press the felt flowers that you rolled up on the glue. Hold this in place and do not let it go until the glue binds it.

- Wait for the glue to dry, and your roses are ready for use.

Custom Coasters

MATERIALS NEEDED:

Free Pattern Templates

Monogram Design (in Design Space)

Cardstock or Printing Paper

Butcher Paper

Lint-free towel

Round Coaster Blanks

LightGrip Mat

EasyPress 2 (6" x 7" recommended)

EasyPress Mat

Infusible Ink Pens

Heat Resistant Tape

Cricut BrightPad (optional) for easier tracing

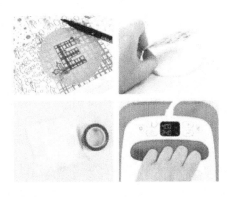

STEPS:

- In Cricut Design Space, open the monogram design. You can click "Customize" and choose the designs that you want to cut out or just go ahead and cut out all the letters.

- Click on "Make It".

- On the page displayed, click on "Mirror Image" to make the image mirrored. This must be done whenever you are using infusible ink. For your material, choose "Cardstock". Then, place your cardstock on the mat and load it into the machine; then press the "Cut" button on the Cricut machine.

- After the Cricut machine is done cutting, unload it and remove the done monograms from the mat.

- Trace the designs onto the cut-out. If you have a Cricut BrightPad, you can use it to carry out this step much more easily, as it will make the trace lines easier to identify. Tracing should be done using Cricut Infusible Ink Pens.

- Use the lint-free towel to wipe the coaster. Ensure that no residue is left behind to prevent any marks being left on the blank.

- Make the design centered on the face down coaster.

- Get a piece of butcher paper which is about an inch larger on each side of the coaster and place on top of the design.

- Tape this butcher paper onto the coaster using heat resistant tape, to hold the design fast.

- Set the temperature of your EasyPress to 400 degrees and set the timer to 240 seconds.

- Place another butcher paper piece on your EasyPress mat, set the coaster on top of it, face up.

- Place another piece of butcher paper on top of these. Place the already preheated EasyPress on top of the coaster and start the timer.

- Lightly hold the EasyPress in place (without moving) or leave it in place right on the coaster – if on a perfectly flat surface – till the timer goes off.

- After this is done, gently remove the EasyPress 2 then turn it off.

- The coaster will be very hot, so you should leave it to get cool before you touch it. When it is cool, you can peel the design off of it.

Customized Doormat

MATERIALS NEEDED:

Cricut Machine

Scrap cardstock (The color does not matter)

Coir mat (18" x 30")

Outdoor acrylic paint

Vinyl stencil

Transfer tape

Flat round paintbrush

Cutting mat (12" x 24")

STEPS:

- Create your design in Cricut Design Space. You can also download an SVG design of your choice and import into Cricut Design Space. Make sure that your design is the right size; resize it to ensure that this is so.

- , you are to cut the stencil. You do this by clicking "Make it" in Cricut Design Space when you are done with the design. After this, you select "Cardstock" as the material. Then, you press the "Cut" button on the Cricut machine.

- When this is done, remove the stencil from the machine and weed.

- , on the reverse side of the stencil, apply spray glue. After this, attach the stencil to the doormat, exactly where you want your design to be; then, pick up the letter bits left on the cutting mat and glue them to their places in the stencil on the doormat.

- Thefollowing step is to mask the parts of the doormat which you do not want to paint on. You can do this using painters' plastic.

- Now, it's time to spray-paint your stencil on the doormat. Keeping the paint can about 5 inches away from the doormat, spray up and down, keeping the can pointed straight through the stencil. If it is at an angle, the paint will get under the stencil and ruin your design. Spray the entire stencil 2-3 times to make sure that you do not miss any part and that the paint is even.

- You're just about done! Now, remove the masking plastic and the stencil and leave the doormat for about one hour to get dry.

314

T-Shirts (Vinyl, Iron On)

To make custom t-shirts using your Cricut machine, you will need to use iron-on or heat transfer vinyl. Ensure that you choose a color that contrasts and matches well with your t-shirt.

MATERIALS NEEDED:

Cricut Machine

T-shirt

Iron on or heat transfer vinyl

Fine point blade and light grip mat

Weeding tools

EasyPress (regular household iron works fine too, with a little extra work)

Small towel and Parchment paper

STEPS:

- In preparing for this project, Cricut recommends that you prewash the cloth without using any fabric softener before applying the iron-on or heat transfer vinyl on it. Ensure that your T-shirt is dry and ready before you proceed.

- On Cricut Design Space, create your design or import your SVG as described in the unit on importing images.

- If you are using an SVG file, select it and click on "Insert Images". When you do this, the image will appear in the Design Space canvas area.

- Then, you need to resize the image to fit the T-shirt. To do this, select all the elements, then set the height and width in the edit panel area, or simply drag the handle on the lower right corner of the selection.

- After this is done, select all the layers and click "Attach" at the bottom of the "Layers" panel, so that the machine cuts everything just as it is displayed on the canvas area.

- You can preview your design using Design Space's templates. You access this by clicking the icon called "templates" on the left panel of Design Space's canvas. There, you can choose what surface on which to visualize your design. Choose the color of your vinyl and of the T-shirt so you can see how it will look once completed.

316

- Once you are satisfied with the appearance of your design, click "Make It". If you have not connected your machine, you will be prompted to do so.

- When the "Prepare" page shows, there is a "Mirror" option on the left panel. Ensure that you turn this on. This will make the machine cut it in reverse, as the top is the part that goes on to the T-shirt. Click "Continue".

- , you are to select the material. When using the Cricut Maker, you will do this in Cricut Design Space. Choose "Everyday Iron-On". On Cricut Explore Air, you select the material using the smart set dial on the machine. Set this dial to "Iron-On".

- Now, it's time to cut. To cut vinyl (and other such light materials), you should use the light-grip blue mat. Place the iron-on vinyl on the mat with the dull side facing up. Ensure that there are no bubbles on the vinyl; you can do this using the scraper.

- Install the fine point blade in the Cricut machine, then load the mat with the vinyl on it by tapping the small arrow on the machine. Then, press the "make it" button. When the machine is done cutting the vinyl, Cricut Design Space will notify you. When this happens, unload the mat.

- With the cutting done, it is time to weed. This must be done patiently, so that you do not cut out the wrong parts. Therefore, you should have the design open as a guide.

- After weeding, it is finally time to transfer the vinyl to the T-shirt. Before this, ensure that you have prewashed the T-shirt without fabric softener, as mentioned at the beginning of this project.

- To transfer the design, you can use the EasyPress or a regular pressing iron. Using a pressing iron may be a little more difficult, but it is certainly doable. Before you transfer, ensure that you have the EasyPress mat or a towel behind the material on to which you want to transfer the design so as to allow the material to be pressed harder against the heat.

- Set the EasyPress to the temperature recommended on the Cricut heat guide for your chosen heat-transfer material and base material. For a combination of iron-on vinyl and cotton, the temperature should be set to 330°F. After preheating the EasyPress, get rid of wrinkles on the T-shirt and press the EasyPress on it for about 5 seconds. Then, place the design on the T-shirt and apply pressure for 30 seconds. After this, apply the EasyPress on the back of the T-shirt for about 15 seconds.

- If you're using a pressing iron, the process is similar; only that you need to preheat the iron to max heat and place a thin cloth on the design, such that the iron does not have direct contact with the design or the T-shirt. This will prevent you from burning the T-shirt.

- Wait for the design to cool off a bit, then peel it off while it is still a little warm.

- Ensure that you wait for at least 24 hours after this before washing the T-shirt. When you do wash it, be sure to dry it inside out. Also, do not bleach the T-shirt.

CHAPTER 5:

Make Money with Cricut Machine

Have you ever wondered, "Could I use my Cricut to make money?"Answer is yes! Discover what you need to know about starting a company with your Cricut Explore or Builder, selling the creations you make.

Were you traveling artisans? You may wonder if there's a market out there for your beautiful Cricut crafts when you make presents for your friends and family — could you really make money with your Cricut?

When you work intelligently and pay attention to licenses and copyright, use your Cricut Explore or Cricut Builder cutting machine, you can completely market the products you produce. This detailed article will help you appreciate a lot of what's going on in marketing your designs from Cricut. Get the best out of 2019's Best cutting tool!

Can I Use My Cricut To Sell Products I Make?

The short answer is YES. You can sell the Cricut products you're making!

In this part, we'll talk about licenses, tips for cost-cutting, adding value to your goods, where to market your pieces, and finally, I'll share some ideas to motivate you to use your Cricut for profit to craft!

Start Here: Do I Want My Cricut To Make Money?

Before you really start trying to make a return from your Cricut, take some time and think about whether or not this is what you really want to do. Here are a few things to comment on:

☐ Since your peers say your ideas are fantastic, are you doing it?

☐ Do you want to sponsor your family?

☐ Or are you doing it on the side for some fun playing?

☐ Are you able to work with difficult clients (there are still demanding clients)?

☐ Would you like to find a job something you want to do?

☐ Are you tech-savvy enough to set up an Etsy or easy website?

☐ Can you know more about online and offline marketing?

☐ Is there room and place for you to start a small business?

☐ Will you love your Cricut crafting? Only enough to do so again and again?

I certainly don't want to dissuade you from starting to make your Cricut money.

Your answers to these questions aren't inherently dealbreakers (though they may be!), but they'll give you an accurate evaluation of how you're going to start a small Cricut company!

All About Copyright

Let's continue with licenses and copyrights. It is the place where you can get the fastest (and where the most money will cost you!) in trouble.

Disclaimer: I am not a lawyer in the field of intellectual property, and this can not be taken as formal legal advice.

The Cricut Angel Policy

You can make stuff to sell under the Cricut Angel Policy if you want to use photos you have found in the Cricut Picture Collection. Carefully read this policy — there's a lot of in there! Several things to note:

☐   Most Cricut Access images are included in this agreement

☐   Makeup to 10,000 products for sale using Cricut images

☐   Do not sell any individual photographs

☐   You will provide a certificate of the copyright for your designs

☐   Do not use approved content, such as Disney, Marvel, or Martha Stewart pictures.

Personal Use Vs. Commercial Use

You can purchase them from online stores if you want additional photos. Don't even import Google photos and use them to do projects — you'll almost definitely be stealing copyrights.

When buying from online retailers, make sure you read the cut file terms of use! Any of the photographs you could purchase contain just a license for personal use. For files that are just for personal use, you can not allow stuff to sell.

You will be offered the option of purchasing a commercial license. Any files can come with a trade license. Write the words all over again!

Licensed Image

Pictures of licensed superheroes (think Frozen's Elsa or Marvel's Iron Man) can be sold on Etsy and in other retailers. These typically violate copyright, and you can find it difficult to use them. My advice to you? Stay a long way from approved fonts and images!

Once again, you can't use Cricut Design Space approved images to sell, but you can use non-licensed images using their Angel Policy above.

Starting A Cricut Craft Business

Well, now that we have got that legal stuff out of the way, let's talk to your Cricut about how actually to make money!

Narrow Your Cricut Craft Niche

A tumbler here, a sign of home decor, holiday t-shirts afterward. You'll end up with smaller sales, the commodity lost, and a disappointed audience.

Then, limit your product range down to one or two products or trends and then NAIL IT. At the convergence between what you want to produce and what is lucrative, I recommend you choose something (see below for pricing ideas). You deserve to love what you're doing — and make your time worth it.

Think "added value" when you're trying to determine what products to produce and sell on your Cricut. It may mean all additions to the line, or just niching down. This way, you can give your company a premium.

For example, many people make signs of home decor — maybe your "thing" includes succulents in paper or hand-painted glitter highlights. Perhaps you hand lettering and turning the lettering into shirt decals.

When you're making tumblers, may they're aimed directly at teachers and come with a gift cardholder. Perhaps your one-size-fits-all shop is full of adorable preemie stuff.

If you're the only one who does it, you should charge extra! It also makes the commercial easy to mark, as you'll see below.

One remember-the the larger the drug, the easier it would be to ship. Perhaps you want to save the big signs of home decor for your nearest craft fair. See the segment Shipping below!

Buy Materials In Bulk

You should buy your products and materials in bulk because you've got your niche down. When you shop in bulk, you can shop more tumblers, or vinyl or mugs at a reduced price. When you're only making "one-off" products, buying in bulk is a lot more complicated.

For example, if you are doing holiday t-shirts instead of purchasing standard iron rolls on vinyl at a specialty shop, you can order and save costs in bulk.

Cricut offers vinyl bulk iron-on and vinyl bulk adhesive.

Quality Really Does Matter

Production of a low-quality product is one of the fastest ways to tank your company. Word of mouth spreads easily, and whether you sell in an online store, you can't adjust the appraisals that you get.

Quality matters

So make sure you can reliably deliver quality goods when you set up your company. If you notice that your efficiency is slipping because you have so many orders, maybe you should pause your shop or recruit someone for a short time to help.

Know what you are doing. Please do it well.

Invest In Your Business….Slowly

You don't want to dump all your money straight away into your company. Start tiny and build a loyal group of consumers and friends who enjoy your company. Tell them for updates. If you deliver a great, affordable, value-added product, they'll start recommending you to their mates. When people keep shopping, and you keep seeing orders from outside of the inner circle, you're on to.

This is a positive indication that the company is finding a competitive demand!

Then continue setting together a small number of your earnings to get your company through. If that's a second EasyPress, another tumbler turner, or Facebook ads, you will start increasing your company gradually.

I still get upset when I see people at art fairs and online trading their Cricut creations for super-cheap ones. I would tell those salesmen don't respect their own time or talent!   So tell me — you will charge what it's worth for your offer! Don't short sell yourself. If you're only barely making a profit (or worse, wasting money!), you'll burn out fast.

One thing to remember: high rates do not automatically mean lower revenue. When you are underpriced, consumers would think that you are offering a sub-quality commodity. Instead, because you charge higher, customers would always believe you are offering high priced items.

Calculate your cost

Pricing is still rough! For your Cricut you want to charge enough to make money, but not so much for your commodity not to sell. To reach the price point that makes sense, you can need to play around with your pricing, but here are some strong guidelines:

Start by estimating the costs. And I mean ALL the expenditures.

Let's presume you're doing hand-painted stenciled Christmas signs. You ought to take care of:

☐   Using the same mat on the Cricut mat and render hash marks on it until it is worthless. It will inform you how many Cricut mat stencils you should make.

☐   A frame of wood carving.

☐   Stencil blank — using the above hashmark form.

☐   Masking tape — Find how much of a symbol to need.

☐   Draw a line on the bottle that indicates how many you are using per symbol.

☐   Keep track of how many signals you can make before they start to wear and tear.

☐   Touch-up paintbrush.

☐   Cricut cutter — keep track of how long it takes to remove it.

Add this, and apply your TIME. Choose an amount you like to make per hour and apply it to the rate of the shipping.

Typically speaking, your sale price should be about two and four times the procurement cost everywhere.

You should always scope out other stores to see if you're in the same vicinity, but note that lower prices don't necessarily mean better.

Collecting Sales Tax

Consult with the municipality to see if income tax has to be collected and remitted. You would likely choose to exclude a part of your taxable income. It is one place you'll like your accountant to work on!

You may want to sell your awesome Cricut designs here so you can make money with your Cricut!

☐ Locally by word-of-mouth.

☐ Local trade fair.

☐ Community church pop-up store, kindergarten, supermarket.

☐ Facebook profile account.

☐ Company Facebook profile.

☐ Facebook groups (be sure you have the moderator's permission)

☐ Via your own online shop:

CHAPTER 6:

DIY Projects

DIY Monogram Can Koozies

Instructions:

1) Measure your koozie tallness and width laying level and choose a fitting size (I picked mine to be 2.5" x 2.5").

2) In your plan space draw a circle that is the size you need your monogram to be (2.5"x 2.5").

3) Add a content box and your instructor's (or whomever you are making the koozie for) initials.

4) Decide on a text style (I utilized Effect).

5) Fit the initials to about the span of the circle.

6) Reduce letters until the point when each of the three letters are relatively contacting.

7) Ungroup letters and stretch center letters to be as tall as the most astounding point on a circle (additionally influence center introductory more slender if should be).

8) Stretch outside letters to be around 75% stature of the center beginning (you will most likely need to thin these letters out as well).

9) Using your Cricut to remove the monogram of Iron On Vinyl (make a point to identical representation so it prints in reverse).

10) Iron on to koozie (for full instructional exercise on the best way to apply press on vinyl see this post).

Add your educators' most loved pop to koozie and a couple of additional for them to appreciate as well.

DIY Baby Milestone Blanket

This DIY point of reference infant cover is so natural to make utilizing the Cricut Producer and utilizing the Cricut EasyPress to anchor the iron-on. Start by cutting your iron-on utilizing the Outline Space document. You'll have to open it on a work area then you can spare it as your own particular document and cut from your tablet or telephone.

Supplies:

Cricut Machine

Cricut EasyPress or Iron

2-3 sheets press on

1 1/4 yard white bandage texture

Cricut Configuration Space document

Autumn in November textual style

Directions:

I cut out each number and I've additionally incorporated the words month and months in the event that you need to include that at the base. When utilizing Cricut Press On, it's imperative to make sure to reflect the picture. You'll put it glossy side down on the tangle and cut utilizing the iron-on setting. Try not to utilize the HTV setting with your Creator. For reasons unknown it is slicing totally through. You simply need it to cut the vinyl and keep the transporter sheet unblemished.

You'll evacuate all the negative space and after that cut every month with the goal that you can space them on your cover. When utilizing the Cricut EasyPress, you require a hard surface and afterward a collapsed towel on that hard surface. You require something that will give a little with the goal that every one of the edges will be safely followed. You know you've gotten an awesome grip when you can see the materials surface.

For Iron-On Lite, you'll require a temperature of 305F and afterward press for 25-30 seconds. Give your things a decent warm up in advance and after you're finished squeezing, turn your material over and press again for a couple of more seconds.

Now you're finished. So super simple yet it requires a tad of investment to get your numbers equitably dispersed and to complete the edges of your material. You'll never need to spend $40+ on a Milestone infant cover again.

These DIY infant breakthrough covers are the best child shower blessings you can give. They're far superior knowing you put your diligent work into something so unique.

Oogie Boogie Treat Packs

Make these Bad dreams Before Christmas enlivened cute gift packs in under 15 minutes with your Cricut.

Supplies:

- Burlap Support Packs
- Black Warmth Exchange (Press On) Vinyl
- Treats/Treats
- Cricut Producer or Investigate Air
- Heat Press or Iron

Directions:

Open Oogie Boogie record in Configuration Space (this is an awesome instructional exercise that demonstrates to well ordered industry standards to transfer pictures in configuration space).

Change the extent of your Oogie Boogie face to accommodate your packs (I made mine 2" tall).

Duplicate outlines until the point when you have the same number of appearances as you do packs.

Load warmth exchange vinyl gleaming side down on light grasp slicing mat and send to cut.

Weed overabundance vinyl from around appearances and separate faces (the fundamental toolbox proves to be useful with this).

Preheat burlap sacks before squeezing (either with an iron or warmth press for no less than 5 seconds).

I found through experimentation that you have to push down longer on burlap to get the vinyl to stick. I've discovered that squeezing at 275° for 45 seconds gets everything squeezed splendidly.

Slowly peel plastic support from the left corner.

Fill your treat packs with fun treats.

Teacher Tumbler Blessing Thought

For this venture you will require:

Images from Configuration Space

black, red, green and dark colored vinyl light grasp cutting mat

transfer tape

tumblers

Directions:

First, you'll open up your plan. TIP: I gauged my glass and knew I had around a 3 in x 4 spot to work with. So I made a square shape that is the correct shape in Configuration Space.

Then I estimated these charming instructor statements to fit perfectly! :)

I erased the square shape, and now it's an ideal opportunity to cut!

I sent everything to my Cricut Investigate Air 2 to do the hard stuff! Cutting! :)

Vinyl arrives in a strong sheet with a sponsorship paper. Your machine really cuts the vinyl, not the support paper. It is anything but a printer, it's a shaper. ;)

The following stage is called weeding. Fundamentally you are expelling all the abundance vinyl from around your plan.

Then you'll put a bit of exchange over your vinyl.

Now, we are prepared to apply the vinyl.

Remove the sponsorship paper, leaving the vinyl on the exchange tape. When you are working with a bended surface work on the center and then out. Rub the center of your decal onto your surface, and after that delicately rub the vinyl down toward the two edges.

Then deliberately expel the exchange tape, abandoning the vinyl.

The apple is simply layered red, green, dark colored and dark vinyl.

Then I filled the tumblers with hot chocolate parcels and chocolates.

Diy Magnet Chore Chart

Materials:

Cookie Sheet (I utilized this two pack – idealize estimate!)

Clear glass marbles with level edge – 1"

Adhesive Magnet Paper (simply ensure it's sufficiently thin to   be cut by your machine.

Printable Sticker Paper

Deep Cut cutting edge

Adhesive Vinyl or Cement Thwart in shade of decision

Transfer Tape

Design Space Task for Magnets and Vinyl

Guidelines:

Open up the Outline Space Task and select to tweak it. You can change the name, text style utilized, and so on in this document before we begin (or include diverse errands).

Follow these guidelines for how to make magnets with Cricut. You can skirt the part about making them and go straight to stage four. In the event that you need to include new errands that I did exclude, you can take after the initial steps to perceive how I did that.

Once the materials have been removed, get rid of the overabundance material

and, utilizing exchange tape, exchange the material to your treat plate.

And presently, you're finished!

Diy Grinch Glasses

These Grinch glasses are anything but difficult to make and ideal for your vacation get together.

To influence the glasses you'll need to begin by painting the stems of the containers with the green paint. You don't have to have it too thick in light of the fact that the sparkle will help cover the glass.

Sprinkle the sparkle on top of it. It's most effortless on the off chance that you do this over a paper towel that way you can simply get the towel when you're set and pour the abundance sparkle back in the jug.

you'll need to remove the Grinch face of vinyl.

Use exchange tape to join the vinyl to the highest point of the glass.

Furthermore, there you have it. I made 8 of these glasses in under 30 minutes (you'll need to give the sparkle and paint a chance to set up for a couple of hours before serving however). The best part is they were plastic so I didn't need to stress over them breaking when and on the off chance that they get dropped.

CHAPTER 7:

Other Projects

Geometric Lampshade Or Hanging Décor

W hile this pendant may look intricate, it is actually an easy design that can add a little modernism to your space. You can use it as a lampshade, or you can add it to your décor for just a design detail. Also, you can consider adding a metallic version on the inside of the white pendant to add a little sparkle and interest to the project.

You'll need:

- White cardstock
- Metallic cardstock, if you prefer
- Ribbon or string
- Hot glue gun

Step 1

In Design Space, go into the library and enter the "Make It Now" unit. Find the project labeled "Geo Ball."

Step 2

Once the project loads, place your cardstock on your cutting mat and send it to score the fold lines.

Step 3

Once your paper is scored, glue the metallic and white pieces of paper together. Begin folding the paper to create the geometric shape. Place a line of glue along one edge and bring the project into its final shape.

Step 4

If you are hanging your pendant, make sure to attach your ribbon or string to the bottom of the shape and hand it from your ceiling!

Takeout-Style Boxes

Yes, you could use the go-to plastic to-go containers, or you could whip up a few custom ones of your own. You can serve leftovers in these simple packages or you can add all sorts of embellishments, like stickers and labels.

You'll need:

- Sticker paper for labels or stickers

- Cardstock

- Hot glue gun or glue dots

Step 1

If you are going to add labels of stickers to your boxes, design them in Design Space with the image or text that you prefer. Consider adding the title of the event and the date to the label so guests know right away how long they have the leftovers for in their fridge. Create a variety of sizes so they will fit over the cardstock boxes you are about to create or other containers you might need to use.

Step 2

Once your stickers or labels are created, send the file to print and cut.

Step 3

Search in the Design Space library the template for Chinese Take Out Boxes and load it into a new workspace. Choose a variety of sizes. Load your cardstock onto your cutting mats and send the file to cut.

Step 4

Fold your cut cardstock along the score lines. Apply glue along the edges to assemble the box and reinforce the seams.

Step 5

If you are adding stickers to your boxes, add them now. For other containers, keep the stickers nearby or apply them onto them as well. You are ready to send your guests away in style now!

Latte Stencil

Up your morning coffee game with a dash of cinnamon or espresso powder over the foam. You can also adapt this to add a dash of cocoa over whipped cream on a hot chocolate.

You'll need:

- Cardstock or vellum
- Coffee in a mug and a dusting material

Step 1

Measure the top of your mugs or your favorite mug you use often. In Design Space, create a circle or shape that will rest over the lip of your mug and add another small circle to the side of it to be the tab that you will hold while the stencil is in use.

Step 2

Write your message or create your image on your stencil. Make sure to center your image in the shape. Send the file to cut on your vellum. Weed the small pieces in the center of your design and peel away the outside vellum or cardstock you do not need.

Step 3

When your latte is ready and still nice and hot, place the stencil over your mug and tap your dusting flavor over top of the stencil. Gently lift the stencil away to reveal your barista design. If you used vellum, wash the stencil off and lay aside to dry for yourfollowing coffee creation!

Felt Owls

You can use these as ornaments or hang around for some fun fall décor. You can also have your kids help you create these adorable pinecone owls.

You'll need:

- Various pinecones washed and air dried
- Felt in various colors like brown, black, white, yellow, and teal
- Hot glue gun
- Ribbon

Step 1

To begin, you will want to design the pieces of the owl face and wings in Design Space. The face is made of two large circles attached to one another. The eyes are two layered circles and the nose is a teardrop shape. The wings are two layered teardrops and can have small circle embellishments. You can also create a stomach piece, which is a circle with small circles inside of it. "Eyebrows" in two wings or a small triangle are also good embellishments to design.

Step 2

Send your images to cut out of your felt. Tape down your felt pieces with masking tape or painter's tape if you want to make sure the fabric does not move around while cutting.

Step 3

Begin creating your pinecone owls by taking the pieces and start gluing them onto the pinecone. Alternate colors and styles to create a little village of owls. Glue a small piece of glue to the top of the pinecones to be able to hang them, if you want, or leave them to set flat on a surface.

Paper Flower Wreath

Decorate your door with a festive wreath. You can make it any colors or styles you want based on your décor and taste. Make sure that when you are selecting your colors that you also choose a color "pop," like the teal color in this example. Also, make sure to make different leaves out of green colors. Your wreath base can be anything like foam or twine. If you have a base that is not attractive, grab some coordinating fabric to wrap around the wreath or make enough flowers and leaves to cover the base completely. You can also add embellishments like beads, buttons, felt balls, and more to your project to take it up a notch.

You'll need:

- Wreath base
- Colored cardstock
- Hot glue gun
- Coordinated fabric, if desired

Step 1

In Design Space, find a variety of different flower and leaf projects. Aim for about three or four different flower designs that are different in size. Try to make as many as possible in different colors and sizes. Follow the instructions for compiling the petals and creating the flowers. Pinch the leaves or fold the bottoms over to add dimension to the leaves. A good goal is to have about 30 different flowers and 15 different leaves to start.

Step 2

If you decided to wrap your wreath with fabric, add a little glue to one end of the fabric to the wreath and begin wrapping it around the wreath and securing the other end with hot glue when it is covered. You do not need to cover the whole wreath with fabric or use it at all, just make enough flowers and leaves to cover any exposed wreath base that you do not want to be seen.

Step 3

Begin adding your flowers to your wreath with your hot glue gun. Make sure you are mixing shapes and colors on your wreath. Once all the flowers are added to your wreath, fill in with the leaves. Add other embellishments if you want. When the glue is dry, get ready to hang your wreath!

Felted Animal Masks

Choose your animal and adapt accordingly. You can make these for a dress-up box or Halloween costume. They are also great accessories for adult themed parties.

You'll need:

- Felt – various colors

- Fabric Glue

- Scissors

- Ribbon or string

Step 1

In Design Space, look through the library to find a mask template for the animal you want. There are typically plenty of options available, but you can also develop your own design if you want. Also, make sure to adjust the sizing of the mask to fit a child or an adult.

Step 2

Adjust your design to reflect the different colors of your mask. This will alert your machine to cut out the shapes from different colors of felt. Send the file to cut when you are ready.

Step 3

Use your fabric glue to attach all the pieces of the mark together. If you decide to use adhesive fabric instead of felt, use transfer tape to help attach all the pieces to one another. Also, the mask should have two holes punched in either side of the mask. If it does not, you will want to add a couple holes and then string your ribbon through to be able to tie it around your head.

If you want to add more design to it, consider adding embroidery, sequins, or glitter to your masks.

CHAPTER 8:

Helpful Advice on Cricut Projects For Beginners

S tarting with a few easy tasks and learning more and more practical skills through each project, you will have much fun and be addicted to your new Cricut Maker (or Cricut Explore) before you know it.

Tip 1: Begin with a ready-to-make project using simple materials

Your first design or artwork will take less than one hour because at first, you will pick an easy task, and Cricut will help you by making your craft in a short time. You should choose a project that is ready to make maybe a love card that uses black and white cardstock only. You should concentrate on cutting machine so that you will not have any mess around because cardstock is so easy to find such inexpensive stuff.

Tip 2: How to play with design space

Don't let the word "Space Model" intimidate you. Just before you get your latest Cricut Maker or Cricut Explore, you will start exploring Cricut Design Space. That's where the first Cricut groups and innovative tools will inspire you. You can find some ideas from Design

Space. Open a project ready-to-make and play around a little with stuff going, try some beautiful colors and fonts.

Tip 3: Get the set of basic tools ready

You don't have to get all the tools to make the first Cricut Maker creation as a novice. Cricut, however, has created some high devices that make it all that much more straightforward. The weeder, spatula, scraper, and tweezers are useful in so many applications like picking up vinyl and complicated paper patterns, adding transfer tape, wiping scraps off the floor, and more.

Tip 4: Use cheat sheets

So many awesome bloggers have posted their free Cricut cheat sheets to make it simpler for us all. As quick guides, do them handy.

Tip 5: Let the prompts guide you

The Cricut smart cutting machine has something awe-inspiring; it guides you through every step from selecting materials to loading mats to using the right blades.

Tip 6: Use the test cut feature

Remember to use the trial cut features given to avoid any damage to your material.

Tip 7: Minimize waste, make the most out of your craft materials

The Cricut Design Space is now brilliant; it will bring all forms back together on the cutting mat so that you will end up with the least amount of waste material. There are other options to reuse the supplies for Cricut crafting. You can also reuse the Cricut transfer tape twice in the DIY double-sided wood wall art with a hand-lettered quotation project below, and it will most certainly go for a couple more times. You may also save vast areas of uncut items left on the mat, such as cardboard or prints, and in subsequent designs, carve out more forms from them.

Tip 8: Making your crafting space a happy place to be

If you are a novice of Cricut Maker or an accomplished craftsman, it's essential to have all the craft supplies and equipment well arranged, so you have joy and consistency in your design room. Lots of fantastic ideas and inspirations can be found on how to organize your Cricut craft room, create a dedicated area for all, and make it appealing as well.

How To Use Ready-To-Make Projects In Cricut Design Space

Ready-to-make projects are just what they sound like, designs already planned, and prepared to be cut without any change being done. To use these templates, you don't have to learn much about the different tools and techniques in the Cricut Design Room. You can simply just pick the one you want, open it up, and submit it to your cutting machine. These templates can also be designed like your designs. Once assembled, you'll have a professional-looking project done in minutes.

Once you open Cricut Design Space for the first time, a menu of Ready-to-Make projects will immediately appear at the bottom of the desktop. During any time, you can also navigate the vast array of tasks by clicking on the "Tasks" button along the left side toolbar. You may also use the Ready-to-Make Tasks menu along the top toolbar to narrow up the quest or navigate by type. There are endless templates online, and you can peruse creative juices through the categories. If you are signed in, you can support any style you want, and you can find it quickly and conveniently far along by clicking in the drop-down menu on "My Ready-to-Make Creations."

Seasonal T-Shirt Designs In Cricut Design Space

Some of the most common things crafters do with their Cricut machines are to make personalized t-shirts, onesies, and other clothes, so you certainly won't be surprised to hear that there are many pre-made clothing patterns in the Ready-to-Make Project catalog. New templates are submitted to the library and every week from sassy sayings to seasonal iconography.

Using Ready-To-Make Projects In Cricut Design Space

As mentioned above, about ready-to-make projects is that if you just want to see how a plan comes together from start to finish, they couldn't be simpler and are perfect. You can customize any Ready-to-Make project to match your style and tastes just as you can any concept you build. Click on the picture after you find a Ready-to-Make plan that you want to pursue in the Design Space catalog. A pop-up window will appear, listing all sorts of valuable details. It not only contains all the materials required to produce the project precisely as seen, but it also gives step-by-step instructions that you can print out and carry alongside you.

Remember that the bottom of the pop-open window has two buttons: a "Customize" button and the green "Make It" button. When you click the "Make It" button, Design Space will immediately forward you to the cut panel. Each of the design components should be designed and colored precisely, as seen in the image shown, and all you need to do is press the green "Start" button to launch the design cut. It is important to remember that you can't change the scale, color, or any other aspect of the design at this point (once on the cut screen). This choice can only be used if the Ready-to-Make concept is to be produced precisely as seen (including completed dimensions).

If you're dealing with iron-on fabrics, you'll need to press the Mirror button on. Cut mat; it won't be done for you automatically! If you click the "Customize" option, however, the pre-made design will be placed onto a canvas of display spaces. You can edit every aspect of the template until here, much as you'd be designing your layouts. You can change the scale, remove items, transfer information, or even switch phrases and photographs if you wish. Those pre-made templates will, therefore, become perfect starting points for your creative creations. Click the green "Edit It" button to return the model to be sliced until you're pleased with the edits or customizations. Every Ready-to-Make project includes guidance on how to cut and build a specific product.

CHAPTER 9:

Working With Images, Text, and Color

To working with images in designing space applications, follow these simple steps. The open space design and click New to create a new project. This will open the enlarged view where you can view images of icons on the left side of the screen. You will be able to see all the images in the Cricut library, search for a specific model, or go to the categories of view. Additionally, you will be able to reach the light of cartridges, where it has more than 400 rounds (image sets) to go through. You can select multiple images and insert them into your project. Once images are loaded, you see the active editing bar, and you can play with the options available in that country.

Text

To add text in the enlarged view, select the text icon in the left panel of this view. Then you need to choose the font you want to use; then you will see the text displayed in the text box. To exit the text box, you need to click outside the text box, and then you will be able to rotate, move, or resize the text. To edit the manuscript, you must double-click the text box, and then you will be able to change the / line spacing, font style or size of the letter, or change the font itself. All these options are available in the edit bar text; you can be seen in the enlarged view.

Color

There are three possible ways to configure the color in an image or object in space design Cricut:

- Basic color unit

- Custom Color Selector

- Hex values

Imagine having an inserted image in the magnified view, but you have to change the color of the layer. To do this, click the layer button on the right side of the screen. You should be able to see the option line type, where you can see the primary colors (must be 30 primary colors), the selector custom color, you can use the mouse to go up and down the stopper for the color you want, or if you are familiar with hexadecimal values, you can enter the amount you wish to in that window. Sounds simple, right?

Printing and Cutting

Strange as it may seem, this machine can print the final version of your project and submit the project to be cut on your Cricut machine. Your laptop or computer is already connected to the printer, so why not print the project completed in their printers? This is why Machine Design Space has the Print option than cut it. You may even prepare the process, passing through printing. Then, cut calibration. For this procedure, follow these steps.

Open space design Cricut, go to the Account menu, and select Print Then cut calibration. Then the window appears for this operation. Select the printer you want to use and click Print. Put the calibration sheet printed on the cutting, placing it in the upper left corner of the mat. Simply click Continue. Make sure the Cricut machine is on and connected to your computer or laptop (via USB or Bluetooth) and select the device from the drop-down menu. Thefollowing step is choosing the right material adjustment, place the plate on the machine, and press Go on the computer.

The machine starts scanning the sheet inserted for calibration marks, then cut around the small square near the center of the sheet. You do not have to download the table but will have to check if the cut plays the printed line. Doing so in the design space, you will need to click Yes and then click Continue to get to thefollowing step.

The machine will start the calibration process cutting along the top and side of the page. When finished, do not download the table, but take a closer look at the lines along the sides and the top of the page. Perhaps, some do not touch the printed copy, but maybe others will. The space design software will ask you which letters and numbers cuts are closer than half of the printed lines. To choose the number of the line that is closer to the centerline, click Start and to select the letter that is closer to the centerline, right-click. When finished, click Continue.

At this point, the machine will make a cut confirmation box around the leaf. When this is done, you can download the mat, remove the calibration sheet, and check the last question in the design space. If you are satisfied with the court, tick yes then keep getting information to the final calibration screen. Click Save and Close to save the calibration settings.

You are ready and ready to go.

Troubleshooting and Maintenance

You buy a Cricut machine to get real use out of it, more or less intensity. Naturally, high usage may encounter some technical problems at some point. Also, it is necessary to keep it in a working condition to benefit from it over and over again.

Length of the blade

You can expect a knife to last between 500 and 1500 individual cuts before having to replace it. Life expectancy depends on cutting materials cutting and settings that are used for cutting these materials. Now you're probably wondering: How do you know when a blade needs to be replaced? To answer your question, you will have to control the quality of the cuts. If you start to see an inferior quality, then this may be the time when you need to replace your blade. Life expectancy is mentioned above for sheets original Cricut, so if you want to maximize the use of a knife, make sure you change your cloth with a layer of genuine Cricut. These cutting blades Cricut replacement may be available at the store of Cricut,

Replacing the cutting blade

Since we mentioned the cutting blade and replacing it is necessary to understand how this process can be done since you probably need to do more or less often depending on how often you are using the Cricut machine. The golden rule of the replacement process is to turn off the computer, and you should never replace this part when it is still on. Just to be sure, you can even turn off the machine after turning it off. After all, these are done; you only need to remove the cutting blade assembly. Thefollowing step is to find the blade assembly and push it, so you can quickly get the blade out of the set (but make sure you gently pull the sheet as it is a magnet that holds it in place).

A placing new leaf, let go of the release sheet, and carefully insert the blade shaft in the hole at the bottom of the cutting blade assembly. You will see how the blade "sucked" it is within the cylinder and is appropriately installed—restarting the cutting blade assembly in the Cricut machine, using the reverse procedure to remove the cutting blade assembly. You need to handle the cutting blades with extreme care, as they are incredibly sharp and can easily get cut. The edges should be kept away from children, as they can be cut with them, but they are also a choking hazard.

Replacing the cutting mat

The cutting mat is the part that will have to change more often when a Cricut machine is used. It can only last between 25 and 40 full cuts until the mat is damaged and must be replaced. Again, materials and configurations that use will impact the life expectancy of this spare part. But there are other scenarios when you need to replace the carpet. For example, when the paper is no longer sticking to the canvas, it must be replaced. You may be tempted to use mats of differentmakers with this machine, but if you want to have the best results, you need to use the original Cricut Mats. Also, you can buy healing Mat Ser, which has a much higher life expectancy compared to standard cutting mats. Just a tip,

Cleaning and oiling your machine

There is no product out there that shows no signs of use, so even the Cricut machine can show such signs. You can collect dust and paper particles, or perhaps fat can accumulate on the track carriage. Cleaning machine is a relatively simple process, but you still need to consider turning off the computer and remove the power cord before cleaning. Spray the cleaning solution onto a soft cloth. If no static electricity of the constitution, which can lead to the accumulation of dust or particles of paper, make sure you wipe with a soft clean cloth. If fat is accumulating in the bar on which the carriage moves, using a cotton swab, tissue or soft cloth to remove.

Now you can check the following instructions, as they will be instrumental in cleaning the machine:

Turn out of your Cricut machine.

Cut move the smart car slowly to the left.

Clean the entire intelligent cutting bar carriage using a tissue.

Cut move the smart car slowly to the right.

Repeat step 3.

Smart move the cutting carriage to the center of the machine.

Place a small amount of fat at the end of a cotton swab.

Be sure to apply a light coat of grease on both sides of the intelligent cutting transport, but also around the bar, to form a quarter ring on both sides of the car.

distribute the fat evenly throughout the bar by moving the smart car cut to the left and then to the right.

If you notice any grease build at the ends of the bar, clean.

Marking machine not working

You may experience problems with dialing on these machines, so you may need to follow the troubleshooting steps you can see below (not

The family includes CRICUT Browse):

When Explore Smart Set dial does not turn on:

When you experience this problem, you must have proof of purchase, any bills or receipts you may have when you purchased the product, but also to prepare a short video of the broadcast. Contact members Attention further assistance, and you may be asked to present the video of the question.

CHAPTER 10:

Drawing and Writing With Cricut

I f you realize me, you already know I love to create drawing designs with my Cricut. You can create hand-drawn accents on all of your Cricut tasks consisting of pen and ink illustrations and coloring web page designs. If you love the look of hand-drawn artwork, however, don't need to attract it yourself, permit your Cricut system, and do the work for you!

Materials you need for this tutorial series

Cricut gadget any of the Cricut discover machines or Cricut Maker has to work satisfactorily.

Cricut design area – It's useful to have a Cricut get admission to account so you can use the fonts and features I am the use of. I could be sharing a selection of canvas layouts, a few include unfastened pictures, and some do now not. You could usually update paid images and fonts with those you already own out of your library.

Cricut Pens - you could use the pen that incorporates the system. I take advantage of the primary black in a maximum of my projects(.3, .Four, or middle of the night are extraordinary). If you would really like it so that it will use the one of a kind sorts of writing, you'll need to shop for the extra Cricut pens and pen units.

USING CRICUT PENS

Permit me to start out via clarifying. I generally draw with my Cricut. I draw a long way extra than I write. So, I tend to speak about "drawing" far greater than I communicate approximately "writing." But, once I proportion those pointers and information, the thoughts generally practice to both drawing and writing. So please remember that if I say drawing, the top will, in all likelihood, work in your writing as well.

You could convert nearly any cut layout to a drawing layout or upload drawing factors to any challenge. I really like to play with the designs and spot what appears suitable as a drawing. Feel unfastened to play together with your cut documents and see what takes place if you convert them into drawing designs. Just remember, what you see on a display screen is usually what you're going to get on paper.

TYPES OF CRICUT PENS

On the whole due to the fact I simply love black line art. So don't fear if you don't have all of the pen sets. Play with the artwork ideas using the pen you have, when you fall in love with the drawing competencies of your Cricut, you may usually buy greater pens!

You could additionally buy a spread of different pens for your Cricut machine.

Trendy pleasant tip pens are available in a wide range of colors. The first-rate point hints are best for adding accents to your paintings or developing drawing best designs. The recommendations are small sufficient to attract pretty small elements, even as growing a pleasant crisp line. I take advantage of the. Three and .4 black tip pens for pretty much the whole thing, inclusive of my hand drawn artwork it's an extraordinary high quality factor black pen. The "midnight" pen is a quality factor.

Glitter pens are more like a ball factor pen with a pleasing go with the flow to the ink, so you get an amusing glitter accessory with a steady line.

Calligraphy pens come in a ramification percent with some different sizes along with up to 2 calligraphy pen nib sizes. This can permit you to create an elaborate calligraphy look to your Cricut pen art.

Metal pens have a piece bigger nib and draw extra like a small marker. Those nibs are the "medium" categorized pens.

Infusible Ink Pens and Markers provide a whole new cause to apply pens together with your Cricut gadget. Infusible Ink is a heat-set ink that permits you to create all types of custom designs on your tasks. Read extra Infusible Ink here.

The Writing Palette

You may pick the coloration you want the layout to show up on a display screen. In case you need all images, as an example, to be drawn with the identical black pen, ensure you are deciding on the equal pen and color desire for every layout on your completed piece.

The most recent model of design space includes a color selection display that lets you pick out a color you've already used without problems. You can nonetheless select a color from the larger shade palette.

While you set your Cricut to create your design in layout space, you'll be triggered to exchange your pen colorations as wanted. Each color you pick out for the layout layers will bring about an on-screen message letting you know whilst to interchange your pen shade even as the Cricut is growing your layout.

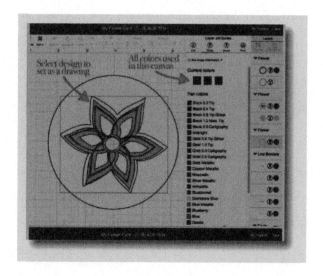

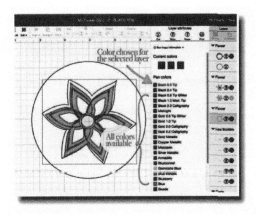

Writing palette options in Cricut Design Space

DESIGNS TO DRAW

The drawn line, in lots of instances, can not be used as a cut shape. See the picture above of the flower? You can convert the reduce line to draw, but if you set the drawn line to cut, you'll emerge as with a bunch of scraps of paper and no longer a quite flower.

To discover my designs, click on "photos" at the left aspect of the display while you are operating on your canvas. Then inside the upper right, enter "correct" inside the search bar. You ought to see all the images to be had that i have created. You could also click on "cartridges" to discover my currently to be had layout units, all of them include pictures created to draw specially.

TIPS: DRAWING AND WRITING WITH CRICUT MACHINES

To maintain a layout together, connect the drawing lines collectively. Grouping strains will now not result in a selected layout. Grouping simply helps you to move the portions around your paintings canvas together.

To dictate in which drawings are positioned for your format, there are two selections.

Connect the drawing to the layout to your canvas layout. I really like to create a heritage paper on my canvas and connect the drawings there.

Take note of how traces appearance on the display screen. How they seem on a display screen is how they will appear on your paper. If designs are overlapping... the pen will draw overlapping strains. Presently, there is no direct way to reduce out portions of lines, so ensure to take note of how the lines appear.

Take a look at the exceptional pen types, so you get an idea of ways dark the colors are and how they appear on different papers. Gold glitter isn't nearly as bold or obvious as gold metal

I've created writing with your Cricut system practice layout canvas you may use to exercise your abilities drawing and writing with your Cricut device. You may play with the one-of-a-kind shapes, exercise switching from writing to slicing to printing, and see the consequences you get.

Greater help AND thoughts FOR DRAWING AND WRITING along with your CRICUT machine

Take a look at the series! I've eventually completed this 12 element collection, underneath you will find a listing of the subjects to select from. Every lesson consists of an assignment canvas you could use through the Cricut layout area to help you practice the strategies AND do an amusing project. I'd love to listen to what you think. Please let me understand if you have any questions otherwise you get stuck along the way. You can also prevent with the aid of the hundred directions Facebook web page and say hey!

The first in this collection is this get began manually with all of the suggestions and tricks you need to get started the usage of your Cricut machine and the Cricut pens. I actually have a primary Drawing together with your Cricut academic as an outline that will help you learn how to upload drawing and writing on your Cricut projects. The series consists of eleven extra instructions concerning unique uses and strategies.

You do now not always need to examine those strategies so as, however, I tried to lay out the various techniques in an easy to advanced order.

Cricut Project Ideas – Using Pens to Add Art Accents

Discover ways to created advanced Cricut task ideas via using Pens to add art Accents. You can upload pretty embellishments and artwork designs to your Cricut initiatives easy by means of such as the pen in your task advent. That is the ultimate lesson in my 12 part collection, gaining knowledge to draw and write along with your Cricut. Add greater layers of shade or suggestions of steel shine to your initiatives. You don't usually want Cricut designs with unique drawing or writing lines, these days, I'll display you how.

Adding accents to your Cricut Projects from Cricut pen

CRICUT PROJECT IDEAS – USING PENS TO ADD ART ACCENTS

Art accents created with your Cricut may be an easy trace of metallic ink or a pretty little glitter line brought to a Cricut challenge. With all the fancy cuts, printed designs, and vinyl, from time to time, only a touch of drawing or writing can entire your undertaking flawlessly.

Many of my personal Cricut designs encompass a drawing specific line only for the motive of adding that extra artwork accessory. However, you don't want a special draw line to add a drawing accent. An easy, transformed reduce line can make a wonderful drawing accent.

You need the following materials:

Cricut cutting device – any version will paintings

Cricut layout space

Cricut pens – your preference

Paper – use practice paper to check out the techniques

Nowadays, we are able to communicate approximately:

- including artwork traces for additional element

- including drawing traces to accent reduce traces

- developing reduce area accents with pens

- including pen drawn text or designs for a non-public touch

- adding artwork traces for an added element

You could add extra designs to tasks the usage of just the pen for small accents of coloration or sparkle. Easy bins or other basic shapes around the artwork in a fun pen ink can add hobby and a completed look in your tasks.

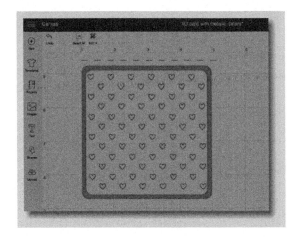

Drawing glitter hearts to create a background

CHAPTER 11:

Cricut Expression

The Cricut Expression is already winning a huge number of awards, gleaming appraisals, and high awards the new Cricut Expression machine is an immense success. Provo Craft has struck it out of the ballpark with this one, and crafters all over the world can hardly wait to get their hands on one of these. What does the Expression machine do precisely? And why are they are so famous?

The first Cricut and the new Expression both are extremely prevalent die-cutting machines. The cut paper, cardstock, vinyl, silkscreens, and substantially more. There is so a lot of you can do with this machine, the conceivable outcomes are huge. There are in excess of 50 diverse Cricut Cartridges to choose from and everyone has several distinct shapes and structures to browse from.

The new Cricut Expressions machine varies from its forerunner in that it has significantly more power and alternatives. It can deal with paper stock that is double the size of the first bug. Every one of the parts is compatible so there are no stresses over utilizing your old cartridges or cutting blade edges. The Expression machine can likewise do various cuts for thicker materials like vinyl and chipboard. The LCD screen additionally gives you a chance to see your design before you print and cut it, saving you painful mistakes and ensuring you benefit from your paper space.

The drawback is that this machine is a lot bigger than the first. It is more diligently to ship to and from your companion's houses, community occasions, and get family parties. It's additionally significantly more costly than the smaller one. Anyway, it offers significantly more adaptability and it can deliver die cuts of up to 24 inches in length! All things considered, this is one astounding machine, and converse with any proprietor to hear how it merits each dollar spent.

Before you purchase it is possible that one think about what you need to do with your specialties and artworks. Will you need to print large-sized shapes, or will the first sizes work fine? What amount do you plan on utilizing the machine? You can really make your cash by sparing materials and time if you utilize your Cricut enough, so maybe the underlying speculation won't be that huge of a deal for you. Likewise, make certain to search for good limits and deals on the machines, if you are a brilliant customer you can get extraordinary deals on eBay and even at the mortar art stores.

Cricut Expression Die Cutting Machine

- A Scrapbooking Tool That You Should Have

Scrapbooking is one energizing paper-art that interests any people of all ages. If you are one of those paper crafters who are intrigued to draft papers in assortment of ways, at that point you may utilize a device, for example, a Cricut expression machine that can help you in making your papercrafts. You'll simply need to pick the correct die-cutting machine that can give you the best finished results.

You'll discover a lot of Cricut expressions in the market these days. More often, these apparatuses utilize the conventional method for cutting paper where the paper will be put on a layout being secured by a board sufficiently able to protect it, and afterward in the wake of having it gone through what they call the 'press machine' which punches out shapes on the paper. This is a successful conventional strategy which can give a lot of impressions for a specific picture at a certain point, however, you may likewise need to investigate certain impediments when utilizing this option.

Since technology is an undying advancement of devices that you can utilize in whatever craft that you should deliver, die-cutting was brought into another level. Presently, you can appreciate Cricut expressions in an increasingly electronic manner. Rather than making utilized of the old and customary dies, you would now be able to utilize Cricut cartridges which resembles a USB flash drive that you can connect to the front of the Cricut expression machine and utilize the stored pictures just as other available information for you.

This time around, you don't need to stay aware of the regular old styles with regards to paper crafting. You can enhance and be increasingly innovative. Since these Cricut cartridges have more pictures stored just as different alternatives for you to utilize like changing the size and utilizing embellishments, you would now be able to make a design format that you can change every once in a while.

This is one extraordinary apparatus and is a must-have for paper crafters such as yourself. You'll simply need to search for the best Cricut expression machine that can without a doubt live up to your desires. With enough research, you will have the option to make your scrapbooking and paper crafting experience more fun.

Scrapbooking is among the most prominent hobbies and for various decades individuals have to indulge the same. Truth be told, regardless of the advent of the Internet and blogging, scrapbooking has endured and the purpose behind this is you won't discover anything as cozy and extraordinary as a customized scrapbook. Truth be told, you can incorporate content units, photographs and anything you like simply like any cutting edge blog. In fact, it might likewise contain any physical things which were a unique piece of your recollections that you want to preserve. This is the fundamental motivation behind why scrapbooking can never be completely supplanted by blogging. With the prevalent Cricut Expression machine, this will make it simple for anybody and everybody to make a scrapbook. Scrapbook involves cutting of paper is a significant part which can be a tedious procedure.

This is the motivation behind why many people consider scrapbooking as an intricate process that can't be all the more further from reality. You can get yourself an astounding gadget called the Cricut Expressions machine which will really assist you with saving a lot of exertion and time when you are cutting for the scrapbook. This machine is fundamentally created by an organization known as ProvoCraft which specializes in providing the various instruments and supplies for the scrapbook.

You will have the option to cut paper in various sizes and shapes by utilizing the various cartridges accessible with the Cricut Expression personal electronic cutter. You should simply embed the paper in the fitting space in the wake of choosing the suitable cartridge and the remainder of the work will be finished by the machine. It is just stunning!

Any scrapbooking lover will be able to disclose to you that cutting paper requires a considerable amount of time and exertion so as to make a unique scrapbook. Using scissors for cutting paper can strain your fingers and hands, all things considered, and this is the motivation behind why the paper cutters are very achievable for individuals who are into scrapbooking.

You can inquire about on the Internet for Cricut Expression surveys in order to settle on an educated decision when really obtaining this astounding cutter. Also, when you make it during Cricut Expression deal on the web, you can land yourself the best deal. Moreover, you can look at the Internet about Cricut Expression machine's best cost. There are various vendors accessible online who offer stunning deals and discounts on the same by which you can profit.

The Provo Craft Cricut Expression Machine Leads the Way in Scrapbooking Die Cutting

Scrapbooking is the process of ordering the entirety of your recollections whether it be from photos, memorabilia, brochure mementos of hair and so on, into a collection, alongside a story, so that in numerous years to come, you or others can think back on the collection and consider the awesome events and relive the memories.

Scrapbooking has become an artistic expression where a lot of people gather scrapbooking devices and make their pages an extraordinary piece of craftsmanship. Scrapbooking die-cutting machines are presently one of the well-known machines accessible to the scrapbooking and art world, which empowers you to decorate your page with shapes and letters cut from different types of material.

Electronic and manual sorts of die-cut machines exist and one of the most mainstream today is the Cricut scope of machines by Provo Craft. Cricut was the innovator of scrapbooking die cut machines that could cut shapes and letters electronically and they stand apart as being one of the machines that chips away at cartridges, so shouldn't be appended to a computer.

The Cricut Expression machine is the highest point of the line scrapbooking die cutter from Provo Craft. One of the primary drawbacks of the first Cricut Personal Cutter was that you could just place in a half 12x12inch sheet of paper to do the die cuts and this was a genuine drag having to have half sheets of paper around consistently. So the producers of Cricut chose to upscale and cause a bigger version where you can now be able to do die cuts with 12x12 and 12x24 inch sheets.

However the Expression machine is much bigger, than the Personal and the Create Machines, that it is unquestionably not effectively compact any longer and is intended to be kept in a perpetual spot in the home, or as Provo Craft are presently focusing on... the school spot or media room!

The Expression has no different incredible highlights of the first Cricut Die Cutting machine. This incorporates the capacity to cut shapes with no computer required. There are heaps of textual styles and designs accessible in the monstrous cartridges selection. Likewise, similar cartridges bought can be utilized over the entire Cricut machine range. It likewise can cut shapes in various sizes automatically without having to watch machine excessively.

Given that the Expression has a similar fundamental functionality and design as the first, it additionally has its irritating clingy mat. However, in the wake of having explored a portion of the other die cutting machines, similar to the Making Memories SLICE, I see this is a slight benefit, as the Making Memories SLICE must be looked after while cutting, as it doesn't have this clingy sheet.

Hopefully, one day Cricut will think of a superior method to enable client cut sheets without holding the paper and without utilizing the clingy mat, because it is real pain, particularly in the event that you need to cut shapes from fragile paper.

The Cricut Expression is likewise the most costly machine as of now available at around US$500.00 RRP, however, simply looking around on the web, you can easily get it from different spots for US$300 in addition to transportation fee.

So if you are a die-hard scrapper with cash to consume!!! or on the other hand you have quite recently been frugal with your scrapbooking so you could put something aside for the Expression (very well done!) then it is really one of the best in the market right now.

Conclusion

Thank you for making it to the end. Now that I have given you several ideas of projects that can be completed with the use of a Cricut, you should have more ideas on how to use your new Cricut machine. Each Cricut is capable of doing some super impressive creative projects.

Never stop doing research. Never stop trying new things. Never, ever stop being creative. The Cricut does not make you any less creative; it just makes the process easier so that you can focus your valuable time and efforts on more important things or personalizing the projects after making the cuts. It takes the tedious work out of your hands and makes everything fun, easy, and fast. One of the greatest things about a Cricut is that it is extremely simple to use. It does take a while to get used to using it, but once you get the hang of it, only your creativity is the limit. With that in mind, this part focuses on giving you a beginner's guide on using the Cricut. Firstly, what comes with your Cricut? That depends on what product you purchase and the money you pay. The more you pay, the more you get. These don't look like a lot of things, but they are all the right ones to get you started. For a beginner, it is recommended that you purchase a starter set which includes the necessary accessories.

The primarily phase in the course of setting up a Cricut is to determine where the machine will be best located. Ideally, the machine will be placed near a computer or tablet, a power source and where it has room to work. Even if the machine does not require to be hooked to a computer, try to keep it within reach to make the process of loading and unloading easier. When you purchase your Cricut machine, you will be excited to get started. Search the online Cricut library for ideas on how to create cool projects that will make your environment more enjoyable, as well as projects that you can use to give others joy in their life such as cards and wooden signs. The great thing about the Cricut is that you can use it with so many different materials that you will never run out of ideas for crafting and creating wonderful gifts.

Now that you have completed this handy manual on how to use the Cricut machine, you should be well-equipped to head out into the Cricut crafting world and start designing your favorite craftstoday. Make Your First Art Sale Online, in the long run, individuals will be keen on your work and can hardly. Finally, if you would like to feed your newfound Cricut obsession, go right ahead and buy one of the newest Cricut Gypsys. This useful, hand-held apparatus will keep your font cartridges ready for simple portable use. It's possible to design from anyplace on the move, in the physician's office, even while on holiday, or merely sitting on your sofa. Anything you plan on the Gypsy is totally transferable to a Cricut device for die cutting. If you save your layout, it may be linked to one of your Cricut apparatus and published at a later moment.

I hope you have learned something!

Made in the USA
Monee, IL
04 December 2020